The New American Compact

Restoring the People's House to America

Stacey Tallitsch

Bloomington, IN  Milton Keynes, UK

authorHOUSE™

AuthorHouse™
1663 Liberty Drive, Suite 200
Bloomington, IN 47403
www.authorhouse.com
Phone: 1-800-839-8640

AuthorHouse™ UK Ltd.
500 Avebury Boulevard
Central Milton Keynes, MK9 2BE
www.authorhouse.co.uk
Phone: 08001974150

First published by AuthorHouse 5/2/2006

ISBN: 1-4259-0181-6 (sc)

Printed in the United States of America
Bloomington, Indiana

This book is printed on acid-free paper.

Signatories

At printing:

District	Firsr Name	Last Name	Street Address	City	State
FL-06	Dave	Bruderly	920 SW 57th Drive	Gainesville\,	FL
CA-49	Jeeni	Criscenzo	PO Box 927	Ocenaside	CA
MI-11	Tony	Trupiano	P.O. Box 723	Dearborn Heights	MI
CD-19	Ben	Shuldiner	PO Box 608	Crompond	NY
TX-06	David	Harris	P.O. Box 1408	Fort Worth	TX
MI-06 '04	Scott	Elliott		Benton Harbor	MI
CA-11	Jerry	McNerney	POB 12022	Pleasanton	CA
	Ben	Shuldiner	P.O. Box 608	Crompond	NY
PA-03	Steve	Porter	9451 Page Road	Wattsburg	PA
PA-19	Joe	Otterbein			PA
FL-13	Mike	LaFevers	8437 Tuttle Ave, Suite 125	Sarasota	FL

Stacey Tallitsch (La-01)
http://www.staceyforcongress.com

Acknowledgments

I want to thank Paul Politis, who edited this book in his "free time" during 3 hectic days. He was the 2004 Democratic candidate for Congress in PA-9. A former journalist whose writings have appeared in a number of publications over the years, he is also a small businessman and progressive activist. He and his wife of 32 years, JoMarie, live in Greencastle, PA. They have 3 daughters and 2 grandchildren.

Thanks Paul.

Also, I would like to thank Cynthia Pooler the founder of November Victory. After spending untold hours as a concerned citizen about the future of the United States, she took it upon her self to do what many in leadership roles could not. She united over 100 congressional candidates from all across the country to talk and discuss what it means to be a Democrat and a responsible leader.

On the next page there is quote from Margaret Mead. Cynthia Pooler not only understands Margaret Mead, she lives the life.

"Never doubt that a small group of thoughtful committed citizens can change the world. Indeed it's the only thing that ever has."—Margaret Mead

Table of Contents

Preface

Why does America need *The New American Compact*?

A wise man once said "As you do to the least of us, you do to me," a concept reiterated throughout history by Gandhi, Martin Luther King and other spiritual leaders, many of whom met death at the hands of those threatened by this vision. As Americans, we should stand up for this concept, not advocate and act toward its extinction.

But that's not the America that's shown itself thus far in the 21st Century. We've elected a Republican majority that consistently and zealously act against our best interests in order to satiate corporate lust, and they've done it with little more than candy corn quotes and bumper sticker philosophy.

John F. Kennedy tried to warn us of this behavior.

> This link between leadership and learning is not only essential at the community level. It is even more indispensable in world affairs. Ignorance and misinformation can handicap the progress of a city or a company, but they can, if allowed to prevail in foreign policy, handicap this country's security. In a world of complex and continuing problems, in a world full of frustrations and irritations, **America's leadership must be guided by the lights of learning and reason or else those who confuse rhetoric with reality and the plausible with the possible will gain the popular ascendancy with their seemingly swift and simple solutions to every world problem.** –*President John F. Kennedy (November 22, 1963)*

While these are the words of John F. Kennedy, they never fell from his lips. These were the words he was going to say in Dallas, TX, but was assassinated en route. The repercussion of that one evil act has echoed into our soul even more today resonate in our hearts.

The GOP Majority is out of control, but their days *shall* come to an end.

If elected, the Signatories, all Candidates for Congress in 2006 that have already signed and those that may sign in the future, pledge to *act* on the 10 articles in this book, in the first 100 days after regaining control of The House of Representatives.

It's time to reign in the greed that's consumed "Representatives" who constantly act only in *their own narrow political* interests, rather than for the real interests of those who elected them, even acting against the religious principles they so loudly proclaim in photo-ops, editorials, speeches and campaign appearances.

Many Republicans have forgotten that they have their job by our good graces, not the other way around. They are not royalty, not divinely chosen, but are merely politicians who've mastered the art of the snake oil salesmen.

When they stormed into Congress a decade ago, taking control of the House for the first time in 40 years, they were a fresh-faced band of ideological candidates brandishing a "Contract With America."

They promised balanced budgets and a restored trust in the nation's elected leaders; they would serve and then return to the private sector. But the GOP document turned out to be a Faustian Contract *on* America. Their leaders were Hit Men and perhaps even the sheep didn't know it.

Their leaderships behavior has shown that charlatanism is the only skill they've mastered; the sleight of hand of the con artist in a shell game.

In the 12 years of Republican majority in the house, the Republican leadership has strayed far from the promises that got them there. The nation has run up record budget deficits and debts and term limit pledges seem little more than a stale joke as the majority repeatedly votes to weaken the ethics-enforcement process in government.

Republicans promised to reduce the size of government and cut taxes. Instead they've quadrupled many areas of government spending, doubled the number of corporate lobbyists in town and cut taxes to those who benefit most from big government -- mega businesses and the super rich. The national purse has been pillaged by billionaires who paid to elect personal sycophants and the government has become devoid of true representatives of the people.

Even stranger, many Americans are shocked that Republicans lied to them. Yet in the last few months a growing mass within that party have begun to realize what's happened.

One can find no better example of a billionaire's sycophant than the recently-deposed House Majority Leader, Tom "I am the government" Delay. The Texan, who proclaims at every photo-op to be a "follower of Christ," was formally slapped down, by the weak House Ethics Committee, three times in 2004 for his mafia-like political fundraising tactics.

His response? The weak punishment "proves" he was innocent.

Meanwhile, under Delay's demands,(no wonder he was nicknamed 'The Hammer)', Republicans have altered ethics rules in the House to limit debate, and increased the number of bills presented to members without allowing any changes. Just two recent examples were the CAFTA and Medicare Prescription Drug votes, in which Republican leaders kept the vote open for an unprecedented 3 hours while they twisted arms to garner enough votes for Delay's pharmaceutical benefactors and slave-labor industries. None but the most shameless CEO's benefited from these bills or Delay's behavior; certainly not the voters!

And what's been the result of all of this?

Our government is broke and broken. The dollar is tanking, the budget deficit and our national debt grow by billions each month, trade shortfalls are so big they can be seen from space and we're increasing dependence on third-world tyrants for our drug-like addiction to petroleum.

Meanwhile under George W. Bush, who bankrupted every business he ever ran. The country has created unprecedented wealth for the super rich, creating the greatest disparity between rich and poor of any major nation. We've sworn to depose tyrants who torture women and children, while bombing women and children ourselves. We demand the rest of the world honor international treaties while we violate or refuse to join international treaties.

Congress has pursued an endless series of pantomime investigations, not of its own dealings, but as a distraction from its actions. Baseball players on steroids became part of the State of the Union Address and the privacy of Terry Schiavo was terribly exploited as a Republican issue in Congress so Republican Leadership could slither around her death bed.

Meanwhile unscrupulous talk show hosts and "columnists" were being paid to spread government propaganda on the public airwaves.

Republicans assured the world that Saddam Hussein was lying about weapons of mass destruction, but in the end made Hussein seem comparatively honest, especially in the Middle East. Meanwhile Bush refused to meet with Cindy Sheehan, the mother of a soldier slain in his illegal occupation of Iraq.

> The truth is we're being looted while Rome burns.

We've blown over $200 billion, lost over 2,000 young Americans dead and tens of thousands of wounded who thought they were fighting a noble war are coming home broken physically, mentally and financially. Republicans have repaid those soldiers by cutting health benefits, closing military bases and hiring mercenary "civilian contractors" at seven times a soldier's pay because they have no accountability to the Geneva Conventions.

Frightening, and sad, is this 21st century Republican attitude that presumes that they are above accountability, has been shared by other tyrants throughout the world's history . . . just before the fall. Shall we be taken down with the ship of state, or will we throw these imposters overboard?

Under Republican ideology, we're well on our way to understanding the shame felt by so many in modern Germany -- a great nation whose leadership acted less like Christ and more like an anti-Christ.

> "We will not be driven by fear into an age of unreason, if we dig deep into our own history and our doctrine and remember that we are not descended from fearful men, not men who feared to write, to speak, to associate, and to defend causes which were for the moment unpopular. This is no time for men who oppose Senator [Joe] McCarthty's methods to keep silent. We can deny our heritage and our history, but we cannot escape responsibility for the result." -- *Edward R. Murrow,* 1954

The Republicans are wrong, and what makes it worse is they know it. Yet they still refuse to change the course of their failed policies.

So we have two options. One is to trust a Faustian bargain with those who made the mess, known as "Stay the Course," or, we can bring in a new Congress dedicated to resolving our problems. The longer we remain frozen in fear and division, the more the greedy can treat our nation's budget as their own personal piggy bank.

When we take to heart the words of FDR, that we have "nothing to fear but fear itself," we can begin the fight to take America back.

It would, of course, be unfair to blame only Republicans for the current state of affairs. Democrats have been complacent and compliant when they should have been standing up and shouting down!

From authorizing the Iraq invasion to sharing in wasteful domestic spending, Democrats have not always been the vaunted "party of the people" of their banner.

> "All tyranny needs to gain a foothold is for people of good conscience to remain silent." - *Thomas Jefferson*

And so the infrastructure of both parties is in need of overhaul. Too many people have paid in blood...and sweat and tears . . . for America's freedom, to allow it to be destroyed by shortsighted, self-serving, privileged egoists.

If they don't like that idea that governance is for the benefit of the people not the government then they can go to prison with the rest of the corporate criminals.

If they are incapable of policing themselves in these matters, it's up to us, the American people, to enforce the virtue of law that Republicans are so eager to void and nullify, unless of course they can profit from it.

It's time to vote your own interests for a change. Encourage your Democratic candidate for Congress to pledge to *The New American Compact*, and bring sobriety back to Government.

Article 1 – War is a last option, not a first choice

Section (A): The Signatories are committed to upholding the virtue of doing unto others, as we would have them do unto us.

Section (B): The Signatories do defend America's people from the roguery of Free Trade, opting instead for Fair Trade, to help level the playing field for honest entrepreneurs and true small businesses.

Many people have asked "what are we fighting for in Iraq" and even more have tried to define the war based on some utopian ideal or personal gain.

The real answer to why we're in Iraq, may be as simple as; it's all about money and greed. Every other reason offered could simply be a pretext to that hidden agenda.

The World Trade Organization's (WTO) Free Trade movement is breeding terrorism. It is a Darwinian business philosophy that seeks to crush those at the lower end of the political and economic food chain.

Republicans like to call it "ownership society."

It's largely because of our support for and promotion of this economic model that the United States is so hated around the world today, especially in many "third world" countries.

It isn't because they "hate our freedom" as President Bush so often claims, but because we continually deny freedom to others around the world for the profit of a few corporations. It's our government's double standard the world hates, not the American people.

The Republican majority supports tyrannical regimes because corporate lobbyists love doing business with them.

These dictators permit slave labor to do the work for these companies, enhancing profits and costing American jobs. When these workers look to the U.S. for help, they find our government and American companies are in bed with the tyrants, and out of anger they fight back. The American public, meanwhile, is generally shocked when oppressed people see us as the bad guy.

> "I hope our wisdom will grow with our power, and teach us that the less we use our power the greater it will be."
> *–Thomas Jefferson*

The GOP Majority in the Republican camp knows exactly why terrorist hate us, but have a flavor-of-the-day blaming system to convolute and obscure the facts. "They hate our freedom," is one of the more blatant lies coming from Republicans.

Why would they lie about such a thing?

Economic inequity is directly responsible for creating the terrorists in the first place as the Fortune 100 sycophants. Their justifications for acting this way are as ludicrous as a drunk who blames the car dealership for his DUI. Yet, they continually get behind the wheel, so to speak, to deal out death, disease and misery as if this is acceptable behavior.

While America is responsible for its leadership acting this way (because the leadership is supposed to represent our desires), Americans are not to blame. We have been intentionally misled as to the goal of the Republican leadership. We have been lied to, marketed to, and fed an endless stream of PR spin to justify corruption and propaganda.

What this means for us is that we are now obligated to purge the liars, charlatans and war-criminals from our government, lest they spread their jaundice deeper into the meat of the body politic.

While the in short-term the WTO seems like it is good for America, this is in fact an illusion. What we do to others, will be done to us, and remarkably by our own hand.

Do not think for one moment Republicans desire anything less than corruption in America. They've got business model's they're itching to instill on American soil.

In the U.S. protectorate of the Northern Mariana Islands (14 islands off the coast of Asia acquired by the U.S. during WWII), Tom DeLay has supported the complete deregulation of all industry. For the workers there, there is now no minimum wage, and no health and safety regulations or benefits. And since these third-world style sweatshops are under U.S. control, all goods manufactured in the Northern Mariana Islands can bear the label, "Made in the USA."

Sweatshops that are forbidden to exist in the USA are legally, allowed to represent the USA.

DeLay's exploitive capitalism is reviled in the Pacific, where conditions for workers are, at best slavery. DeLay would jump at the opportunity to the same business model to American workers in the United States. DeLay seems to consider Union busting a sport.

Sweatshop owners from Hong Kong and the Philippines have quickly set up their slave trade with "guest workers," in the Mariana Islands who are promised a better life in the land of milk and honey in the United States. However, they never touch American soil. These slaves either perform in the factories, or are a part of the black market of sex slaves, where they serve wealthy men in their guest house or hotel rooms.

It's no coincidence that in the Philippines, Al-Qaeda and other terrorist networks are not only thriving, they have all but consumed the region.

The so-called morality of the Republican leadership is a mile-wide, but only an inch deep. What's sad is their shallow sense of morality is being done in our name, the name of The Untied States of America founded on the principal of freedom and free expression.

Human Rights groups have long been upset over Tom DeLay's vision of paradise in the Mariana Islands, complaining that the sweatshop owners become quite displeased when the women "guest workers" got pregnant, because they had to set up a clinic to produce forced abortions. This is a development that would cause DeLay some stress, if it weren't for the fact he wants to abolish abortion in the United States, yet finds the practice totally acceptable for human property. Hypocrisy is the norm in his world and seems to be in the world of the Republican Leadership.

Although DeLay's utopia is not without self-contradicting setbacks, he has his mind set on how things should be in the New National Order, and contradictions will most likely disappear from the minds of people once adequate spin is applied. DeLay not only includes sweatshops for blue collar workers in his own mind, but would like the outlawing of unions all together.

In a letter he sent to the Religious Right PAC, the National Right to Work Legal Defense and Education Foundation, *which promotes the exact opposite of its namesake*, DeLay said that "union bosses" are the real terrorist.

"The union bosses' drive to use the national emergencies we face today to grab more power," Delay said, "...presents a clear and present danger to the security of the United States."

DeLay, a natural totalitarian with apparently fascist instincts and aims, would have trouble with any sort of leaders in a democracy. However, it would appear that those who actually work for a living are putting up some resistance to DeLay. There are many unhappy people in places of work today.

The older workers remember how it was in the 1970s, before Reagan, Bush One, Bush Two, and Tom Delay—and tell of the loss of workers' rights, the better working conditions they had, the right of collective bargaining, and other rights and conditions that have been damaged or eliminated by the Republican Party.

The Republicans want to turn America into their perfect Darwinian business model derived from the Mariana Islands where slave labor is the standard. It could an economic fact however, the result will be our daughters and grand-daughters may be forced to prostitution just to get by financially, a benchmark which can be seen in every country that embraces slave labor. Think about it for just a moment, what would you do if someone tried to enslave you and your children for their selfish profiteering?

Some Republicans are doing it whether you like it or not. And, through our complacency, we are accountable for the destruction of our families—unless we move on Republicans to be removed in as large a number as possible.

But, be warned! If you intend to protect your family from these Republican efforts you are now a "Terrorist" for daring to fight for your rights and the rights of your children. In fact, many Americans are labeled as terrorists by the Republican majority, although they used to be called Labor Unions, according to Majority Leader Tom DeLay.

Republicans have gone unchecked and staying true to form, are totally out of control. What can you do about it?

Support good government, not greedy government.

Today, the WTO is actively trying to undermine the United States economy. For the first time in decades, retailers, apparel firms and others can import unlimited quantities of clothing, sheets and other items from China, India and other slave-labor countries. This action has decimated the economy in the south where cotton and other textile industries reside.

Does the Republican majority care?

Nope, the Republican leadership figures these so-called "Red States" are Sheep and will believe whatever they are told…it's Saddam Hussein's fault, or it's Weapons of Mass Destruction.

The GOP Majority truly has no shame at all.

In truth, some Republicans, many far behind the public scene, don't want to defeat terrorism, as it has become quite profitable. They fancy the idea of handing trillions of our tax dollars in no bid contracts to corporations in which they own shares, hidden from the IRS through blind (wink-wink) Trust Funds and off-shore accounts.

Don't believe it?

Why then is there a newly built community in the Cayman Islands, with no living there, called "Republican Row?" Why do Republicans do so much fund-raising with CEO's there?

Could it be a sanctuary for an engineered Enron style collapse of the United States, with a Republican leadership holding all our money, while they sip Pena-Colatas from coconuts?

If you still doubt, just look at how weak the dollar is against the Euro and you've got 90% of the big picture. Perhaps some in the private Republican leadership want to turn the United States into a third-world country. They've learned how to gain the largest profit when all labor laws have evaporated, because no one is working and people will do anything to feed their children.

Republicans have mastered the Darwinian business model and see the middle-class as its biggest threat. In the world of Darwin, its kill or be killed. You're either rich or you're poor, you control everything or you control nothing.

The middle-class convolutes this Darwinian model by creating moderation between super-rich and super-poor. In turn, this creates serious frustration for the uber-wealthy because the middle-class has a lot of money they can't touch, at least while the dollar is strong.

Bill Gates, the world's richest person with a net worth of $46.6 billion, is betting against the U.S. dollar.

"I'm short the dollar," Gates, chairman of Microsoft Corp., told the World Economic Forum in Davos, Switzerland in early 2005. "The ol' dollar, it's gonna go down."

By engineering a weak dollar, your money becomes worthless with an inflation rate out of control. Those immune are those who've changed their portfolio to a stronger currency (euro) or into the gold standard, out of reach from the IRS of course.

It must be remembered that George W. Bush has bankrupt every business he's ever been in control of, and amassed a sizable fortune doing it.

"It is a bit scary," Gates said. "We're in uncharted territory when the world's reserve currency has so much outstanding debt."

Bush has pledged to clamp down on spending to halve the budget deficit -- $427 billion in his first 12 months of the second term through Sept. 30, 2005, but the World Economic Forum in Davos balked asking for a "credible" plan.

Gates reflected the views of his friend Warren Buffett, the billionaire investor who has bet against the dollar since 2002. Buffett said last week that the U.S. trade gap will probably further weaken the currency.

"Unless we have a major change in trade policies, I don't see how the dollar avoids going down," Buffett said in an interview with CNBC Jan. 19, 2005.

Who's in control of the United States trade policies? Of late, it has been the faceless directors of the World Trade Organization (WTO) which has no allegiance to any country or form of government, only the Darwinian business model.

It's how the super-wealthy shift the greatest amount of wealth into their pockets, offering them greater control over a limp or even collapsed country.

This is not theory. It's a model that has been tested all over the world with huge success. Hitler used it during his rise to power with the help of the industrial complex, which it must be added, happened to be the Bush family two generations ago.

How do you think we beat the Soviet Union with George H.W. Bush as Vice President? We didn't out spend the Soviets—we destroyed the value of their currency. How are things working out for Russians today?

In an America as divided as it is, do you really think it can survive a Soviet style collapse?

> "A house divided against itself cannot stand." –*Abraham*
> *Lincoln, June 16, 1858*

Don't worry; theocrats are waiting in the wings to come to our "rescue." Isn't it nice to know the "Party of Morality" and Family Values® are seemingly working so hard to undermine the United States for selfish profiteering?

What does that mean for the rest of us, who don't make $7 million or more a year?

If you think your rights are secure in a defunct government, just ask the people of Iraq how well their civil rights are being respected. Iraqi's had more rights under Saddam Hussein.

Think of what kind of laws the American Tele-Ban of Rev. Jerry Falwell, Pat Robertson, James Dobson would promote. Women's rights would be an oxymoron, gays would be exterminated, and the days of Jim Crow would look like a utopia in comparison to the reality. And forget history, only sanctioned scripture would be allowed in our schools promoting the Flat-earther ideology of a 6,000-year-old Universe, if we had schools at all.

Basically, we would be like the Middle East, a Republican paradise on earth. A world the Founding Fathers went to war to prevent, where lords and surfs are ranked by the "ordained order" of tyrants. And, dare to argue "that all men are created equal; that they are endowed by their Creator with certain unalienable rights" and you've just become a "terrorist," while Republican sycophants live the life of luxury in the Cayman Islands.

This is the world if Republicans are allowed free reign on Free Trade, where Darwinian business, corrupt government and the extinction of human rights go unchecked.

The scary part is the GOP Majority is closer to achieving their goal than you think. The very events of 9/11 have created an environment where all the rules of American virtue have been tossed out the window with the code words "post 9/11 world" giving way to some enormously large pigs at the trough.

Most of the educated in the Middle East recognize these problems in their country, and for the most part, are warring against those who are trying to prevent democratic reforms. It just so happens, the leadership in the United States is siding with the Sheiks, and the Mullahs, because Democracy in the Middle East is bad for business, despite claims from Washington DC.

The GOP knows that just because a country has a democracy doesn't mean they become friends to the United States. In fact, most democracies around the world don't like us very much at all. Democracy in the Middle East is a worst-case scenario in terms of public relations, especially since we have armed their oppressors who kill their families and step on their necks.

Republicans lie when they say they are fighting for democratic reforms in the Middle East. In truth, Republicans have become proficient at instilling puppet-dictators who hide behind the mask of Democracy. Republicans put Saddam Hussein in power in the first place, and held "free elections" too, if you remember, and an amazing unanimous consent was the result.

Why would Republicans commit fraud on this level?

Free Trade is a top-down divine business order and once people have a say in their government, (bottom-up) the Darwinian business model begins to collapse.

Why?

The corporate world is, by law, acting in its best interest, not ours. Democracies act in our best interest, not theirs.

To combat that problem, Fortune 100 companies instill puppet politicians who in turn, undermine and dismantle the government from within, by acting in the interest of the 1% instead of the 99%. A process that is repeated all over the globe until the people rise up against it, known to us today as "terrorists." It is quite certain, if Jesus Christ came back today, he too would be called a terrorist for throwing out the moneychangers.

Article 2 – Good Government NOT Greedy Government

Section (A): The Signatories will not sign a Declaration of War without a clear and present danger to the United States. This danger must be proven beyond a reasonable doubt based on facts, not hyperbole.

Section (B): The Signatories will bring those responsible for War Crimes to justice, regardless of class or office, based on the War Crimes Act of 1996.

Long before the fraud of Weapons of Mass Destruction came to light, we knew something was wrong with the War on Terror. It was as if something nagged at our vary soul, like the sound of buzzing locus in the back of our minds.

Maybe it was discomfort over the idea of invading a country that has never attacked us, or with the froth-at-the-mouth hysteria of dubious oil barons. Perhaps it was the flavor of the day justification for invasion (WMD, Human Right, and Non-compliance to UN). Possibly we knew we were being lied to, but either couldn't pin-point it, or didn't care, maybe even a little bit of both.

Something about the War on Terror was terribly wrong, and in the end, history will judge us by the effects of our actions upon others around the world.

Whether the reason for fighting a war was just or unjust, the damage we do to innocents in the process, still matters.

> The end does not always justify the means, nor can justification be snatched at the end.

War Crimes Act of 1996 (as amended)

18 U.S.C. § 2441. War crimes

(a) Offense.—Whoever, whether inside or outside the United States, commits a war crime, in any of the circumstances described in subsection (b), shall be fined under this title or imprisoned for life or any term of years, or both, and if death results to the victim, shall also be subject to the penalty of death.

(b) Circumstances.—The circumstances referred to in subsection (a) are that the person committing such breach or the victim of such war crime is a member of the Armed Forces of the United States or a national of the United States (as defined in section 101 of the Immigration and Nationality Act).

© Definition.—As used in this section the term 'war crime' means any conduct—

(1) defined as a grave breach in any of the international conventions signed at Geneva 12 August 1949, or any protocol to such convention to which the United States is a party;

(2) prohibited by Article 23, 25, 27, or 28 of the Annex to the Hague Convention IV, Respecting the Laws and Customs of War on Land, signed 18 October 1907;

(3) which constitutes a violation of common Article 3 of the international conventions signed at Geneva, 12 August 1949, or any protocol to such convention to which the United States is a party and which deals with non- international armed conflict; or

(4) of a person who, in relation to an armed conflict and contrary to the provisions of the Protocol on Prohibitions or Restrictions on the Use of Mines, Booby-Traps and Other Devices as amended at Geneva on 3 May 1996 (Protocol II as amended on 3 May 1996), when the United States is a party to such Protocol, willfully kills or causes serious injury to civilians.

War must always be waged when a clear and legitimate danger presents itself. The Democratic Party is a party that stands for National Security and our history proves this to be true.

Yet this simple definition of a 'clear and present danger' has been lacking in the Republican mantra for war. They lay claim to 9/11 as the reason for everything, except of course, sending *their* kids into combat. They have better things to do than to risk their lives for a war they started.

No, in the Republican mindset, it is the "colored kids" and the "poor" and the truly patriotic who get to risk their lives, not the silver-spooned trust-fund babes of CEOs and self-righteous politicians. In their minds, the backbone of America must do the bidding of cowards, chicken-hawks, and draft-dodgers because quarterly profits are not as chubby as was hoped.

It's quite a game when you think about it. Increase your profit margin with an army you don't have to pay for, get paid by that same military through no-bid contracts, and get the booty for a song. And the Republicans in the House have found an old saying to be truer than they knew:

> "He who permits himself to tell a lie once, finds it much easier to do it a second and a third time till at length it becomes habitual." *–Thomas Jefferson*

It has taken more than two thousand years for the noble concept of Democracy to resurface, after the tyranny of "Divine Right" and the Inquisition. The Founders of this country started something no *one* thought could be achieved on American soil. Their vision turned out to be, in fact, the flashpoint *for a change in governments around the globe.*

Was that flashpoint an unintentional result?

Yes, but the result was also a predictable one. The people, worldwide saw corruption in their leaders and expunged it from the face of their countries.

Yet a class of cowards has orchestrated this lust for wealth. Most of them never served in the military, and they lead a President who never held a job, never ran a successful business and never even held political office until he was placed in the Texas Statehouse by shadowy groups with power yet unchecked.

They place greed over a world of caring, sacrifice and sharing, and further points up this obvious failure and carry it to the next generation.

It's all perfectly legal in America right now.

The question is:

- SHOULD those who suffer from these malfunctions of greed and contempt for others be given the national purse?
- SHOULD apocalyptic utopians be given the nuclear launch codes?
- SHOULD those who have such little understanding of, and regard for, language and truth be allowed to speak for us?
- SHOULD those who pathologically lie, cheat and steal for their own personal wealth, be trusted to determine our futures?
- SHOULD those who wouldn't be comfortable in our daily lives, be allowed to say they're "one of us" when running for office?

This nation was given to us as our birthright, "We the people," not the corporations, the televangelists, the "think" tanks. We decide who represents us, not them. Because *they* don't!

We *all* get to decide who represents our best interests, not the wealthiest one percent alone. And so we can decide when we've had enough waste . . . of money *and* lives . . . and fraud and corruption and cronyism.

And WE, the people, can decide to throw the corrupt and the evil out of office and into prison.

The only thing we have to do to stop all of this is just say, in one resounding voice, "NO MORE!" Simply: "NO MORE!"

Let's throw them out of office and *elect a new Congress* that will act on our behalf, not on behalf of paper entities, or theocrats, that have nothing but contempt for real Democracy.

Article 3 – We live in a Republic not a Reprivate

Section (A): The Signatories shall defend America from Corporate controls over our voter rights, worker rights and social and economic programs. We also pledge to treat business as business, not as an entity with the same rights and privileges as an individual American citizen.

Section (B): The Signatories shall defend America from corporate piracy and fraud through the virtue of fact-based results, not special interests. Including, but not limited to, a U.S. Constitutional Amendment guaranteeing every living persons right to vote.

Section C: Voter-verified, auditable paper trails must be mandatory in every polling place in America.

1. Elections officials must be non-partisan.
2. Private companies may not run our elections through secret, proprietary, uninspected and unsecure software.
3. Voter suppression, intimidation and gerrymandering of electoral districts for pure partisan gain must stop forever.

According to a July 28th, 2000 article in USA Today, back in 1978 when President Bush was running for congress in Texas, "he predicted Social Security would go broke in 10 years and said the system should give people 'the chance to invest money the way they feel' is best."

According to Gary Ott, who was then a reporter for the *Plainview Daily Herald*, Bush stopped by the paper's little office "maybe five or six times. He'd sit down at my desk; he was a fun guy. He was very outgoing, very friendly, and we would argue politics since I was a liberal. We'd argue over Carter policies." Bush criticized energy policy, federal land use policy, subsidized housing, and the Occupational Safety and Health Administration ("a misuse of power," he said), and he warned that Social Security would go bust in ten years unless people were given a chance to invest the money themselves."

Since 1978 when Bush predicted Social Security would go bankrupt by 1988, the error is proven clear. Today Bush is just plain wrong.

The privatization of Social Security is a horrible idea, and the Republicans know it. However, they're too busy wrangling their hands to care, and are constantly thinking of new ways to scam the population.

To give an example: Bush, in many a speech on Privatization called for Social Security to be put into "private accounts" for the younger generation. Then one day, some focus group showed that people, particularly older people, react negatively to any connection between "Social Security" and the word "private." For some reason, people like the sound of "personal accounts" better than they do "private accounts."

Guess what? The Republican machine (overnight) changed their linguistics for Privatization of Social Security to "personal accounts®." Then adding insult to injury slammed the media for not locking in step with this rhetoric as proof they were the "liberal media." Despite Bush's ad nausea use of the phrase "private account" up to that point, makes no difference. Pharaoh Bush's Dyslexicon is the yardstick by which all language should be measured.

> "I think it's a nutty idea to fool around with the Social Security system and run the risk of [hurting] the people who've been saving all their lives.... It may be a new idea, but it's a dumb one."—*George H.W. Bush*, (41st President and father to George W. Bush) November 23, 1987 issue of *The New Republic*.

Even his fathers considered choices, after a lifetime of public service and a previous Presidency, make no difference to a President and White House leadership that believe they're guided by a divine power and are answerable to no one.

In Republican rhetoric, privatization is designed to "save and strengthen Social Security." This is a lie and they know it, the agenda is to replace Social Security with corporate insecurity. Rep. James McCrery (R-LA), chairman of the House Ways and Means Subcommittee on Social Security, admitted that diverting money from the Social Security trust fund into private accounts will undermine the program. "That is true on its face. It does decrease the level of the fund," he stated. An "anonymous" senior White House official candidly admitted that the president's privatization scheme "would do nothing to solve the system's long-term financial problems," according to the LA Times.

These are the acts of a charlatan. Republicans are trying to stuff an already bulging pocket through the philosophy of the Tyrant.

> "No people ever recognize their dictator in advance. He never stands for election on the platform of dictatorship. He always represents himself as the instrument [of] the Incorporated National Will. ... When our dictator turns up you can depend on it that he will be one of the boys, and he will stand for everything traditionally American. And nobody will ever say 'Heil' to him, nor will they call

> him 'Fuhrer' or 'Duce'. But they will greet him with one
> great big, universal, democratic, sheep-like bleat of 'O.K.,
> Chief! Fix it like you wanna, Chief! Oh Kaaaay!'"—
> *Dorothy Thompson, 1935*

Republicans would like to turn our Social Security trust fund, which by law is *not* the government's money—it's ours, into the Wal-Mart model for a benefits package.

Wal-Mart brags about the generous benefits package it extends to employees. But the company fails to mention in their propaganda campaign (to balance Machiavellian business practices) "only 40% of the company's one million U.S. employees are currently enrolled in its healthcare plan, leaving close to 600,000 of its employees acquiring health insurance elsewhere — or not at all" as reported by Melissa Schorr in the medical journal *Medscape*.[1]

Part of the reason behind this embarrassingly low uninsured rate in the world's only Super-Power Big Box Store (the national rate for insured employees at other large companies is 66 percent) could be the obstacles Wal-Mart places in front of workers seeking access to the health care plan. In spite of an astounding *60 percent annual turnover rate for its employees*, the waiting period for enrollment eligibility was increased to six months for full-time employees and two years for part-time employees. If part-time employees make it over this hurdle, they still cannot buy coverage for spouses or children. It's also a wonder why their employees would even want to sign up for the health insurance plan as Wal-Mart "shifts much of the health care costs onto employees."

It is sad the very name of "Wal-Mart" has become synonymous with "slave labor" throughout the world. The Republican error is unmistakable in both a functional democracy and biblically.

Although, it is fun to watch relatively famous Republican hypocrites quote the whole "eye of the needle...camel" thing with some rather amazing scriptural contortionism. The fact still remains in the end—the Republican mindset with justifying "greed is good" is destroying America, they know it, and still don't care.

As Americans we need to understand, every time a Republican votes to "privatize" our trust funds (Social Security, Fanny Mae, etc.) they're voting give *our money* away to corporations – without accountability. Every time a Republican votes to "privatize" our water supply, he's voting give *our water*, our most precious natural resource, to corporations – without accountability.

Yet, the Wal-marts of the world seem to think they "are people too." As journalist Thom Hartmann observed, "...corporations are asserting that they...should stand side-by-side with humans in having access to the Bill of Rights. Nike asserted...that these corporations have First Amendment rights of free speech. Dow Chemical...asserted it has Fourth Amendment privacy rights and could refuse to allow the EPA to do surprise inspections of its facilities. J.C. Penney asserted...that it had a Fourteenth Amendment right to be free from discrimination—the Fourteenth Amendment was passed to free the slaves after the Civil War—and that communities that were trying to keep out chain stores were practicing illegal discrimination. Tobacco and asbestos companies asserted that they had Fifth Amendment rights to keep secret what they knew about the dangers of their products."

This would be funny if corporations weren't more than happy to deny those very rights to their employee's. In that light, their arguments are beyond ridiculous.

In 1873, less than ten years after the Civil War's freeing of the slaves, Corporate CEO's decided to use the *Emancipation Proclamation* as justification for corporations to declare themselves a "personhood." They believed that, they too, were the victims of slavery and deserve all the rights and protections of the Constitution.

As ridiculous as this may sound, the Supreme Court has repeatedly upheld that Corporations have a 14th Amendment right to do as they please. How strange it is then that in 1886 a Supreme Court opinion would establish the principle that the 14th Amendment makes Corporations "persons" for purposes of Constitutional interpretation. The opinion gives no guidance to the reason for this principle. The question was not even argued since Chief Justice Waite announced at oral argument that "The court does not wish to hear argument on the question whether the provision in the 14th Amendment to the Constitution, which forbids a State to deny to any person within its jurisdiction the equal protection of the laws, applies to corporations. We are all of the opinion that it does."

Corporations have no soul to save, nor any body to incarcerate, yet an old-court still bitter on freeing the slaves it fought to keep, set its bigotry loose on us all.

The argument Republicans often use to nullify full blown riots over this false status of a corporations personhood is "Yeah, but corporations can't vote." This gives the illusion that not all Constitutional provisions are allowed to the paper-entities and everyone should just calm down.

The reality, real people don't have a Constitutional right to vote either. Nowhere does our Constitution say we have the right to vote, only that the States may determine how those votes are cast. The Voting Rights Act of 1964 corrected this error, but as of this writing, *Republicans refuse to renew the legislation.*

In fact, the 2000 Supreme Court decision of Gore v. Bush spelled out in a very loud and resounding voice, that citizens do not have the right to vote. To say otherwise, would mean that the average of 2% of the American electorate whose vote is voided due to errors (wink-wink), and not allowed to recast a correct vote, have had their rights violated. The government, whose tireless vigilance for the rights of the average American (wink, wink) finds that counting every vote is too cumbersome and should be tossed out like rubbish. This error needs to be corrected. First we declare in a Constitutional Amendment, Paper Entities are not real people and thus are not afforded the protection of the Constitution, (as is the standard in every other country in the world) and second, that real people have an undeniable right to vote.

Article 4 – Security: National, Social, Personal

<u>Section (A):</u> The Signatories pledge to hold our nation's security in the highest regard for its people, not for the greatness of an Empire. Our national interests shall be limited to the health of the nation, but not at the expense of human life around the world.

<u>Section (B):</u> Public schools should provide adequate and appropriate academic, vocational and character education to give America's children the tools they will need to succeed in life both financially and as good citizens of their communities and society in general.

The perception of America is that we are the only "superpower" left standing. The reality is that while our military is stronger than the rest of the world the United States is in a weakened state. We are in debt up to our eyeballs, the burden of taxes falls on our middle class, not on those who reap the largest benefit. We have a corporate mindset that says "profit" is a right ordained by our creator. Our population is aging and the future of this country, our children are suffering.

Our Education System is in crisis. This is not an accident; the Religious Right and Sycophants in Congress have engineered it. Televangelists and Politicians who have little or no formal training in education are trying to tell teachers how to teach.

> "No nation is permitted to live in ignorance with impunity"
> –*Thomas Jefferson*

In poor neighborhoods burdened with financing the bulk of their local schools, the institutions have been outfitted to resemble our prison system. Armed guards patrol the halls and students understand that they have no Constitutional rights on school property, even if it is public property no less. They are subject to any kind of intrusive search, abuse or detention based upon the discretion of un-elected officials. The equipment students are given for learning, like computers or classroom size, is equal to their economic class, where an unconstitutional "separate but equal" philosophy is applied to budgets instead of people directly.

This is wrong!

As Americans we have a right to an education in the big cities as much as suburbia does. The economic relation of the community should not relate to our learning institutions. The greater the level of education, the stronger the community becomes, a fact proven by the adequate funding received for the schools in the suburbs of every major city in America.

Televangelists see this failing as a sign to attack the weakest among us, our children. These Televangelists want to build institutions that promote their myopic view of the world and want us to pay for it. They say the system is too far-gone to be repaired and its time to try something new.

Under the banner of "Vouchers" private religious schools seek to decimate our education system by creating an even larger privatized "Separate but Equal" system that leaves inner cities in bigger trouble.

This system is destined for failure. In Louisiana there are more private schools per capita than any other part of the country. **Yet, Louisiana's schools are ranked 49th in the country.** While the private schools in the state do have a higher standard than public, the private schools are committed to profit, not children, where the best looking product wins the day. Admittedly, Louisiana has said of itself as having a "brain-pool crisis." The brightest and most energetic leave the state for greener pastures to raise their own families. The private schools have failed to provide an alternative, they are not held accountable, but still make a pretty penny.

If the determination of a country's future is measured by how it educates its children, the United States is a generation away from third-world status.

But don't you see, that's the whole point. A good education has been the bane of the Religious Right since time immortal. Of late, the tactic called "the wedge" in the upper echelons, but ironically called "intelligent design" in public, is being waged on our children.

For years now, the Religious Right has been trying to convince the rest of us, "Intelligent Design" is merely a theory to explain the unexplainable. They've said that it's not about "God" or "Jesus" it "could mean anything" including Alien abduction. Apparently, that's what has been missing in our children's education, not math, science, reading, and computer skills. Nope, it's truly understanding (or lack thereof) flat-earther science that has held our children back.

The Religious Right says that Darwin's theory of evolution "is just a theory, not fact."

So is Isaac Newton's theory of "Gravity." However, to thrust that into the debate is open that old wound of the pagan "Round Earth" theory.

In Dover, PA the school board decided, despite public outrage, they were going to single handedly preach religious dogma in public schools through "intelligent design." The voters punished the board by removing every single one of them from their post.

> Rev. Pat Robertson, *700Club* mullah, declared a fatwa on the town of Dover. "If there is a disaster in your area," he said, "don't turn to God — you just rejected him from your city. And don't wonder why he hasn't helped you when problems begin, if they begin. I'm not saying they will, but if they do, just remember, you just voted God out of your city. ... Don't ask for his help, because he might not be there."

At the same time voters in Dover were standing up for common sense, Kansas' state board of education was voting to adopt standards undermining the teaching of Darwin's theory. This is the latest step in the state's long, hard-fought campaign to turn out stupid kids.

However, the Republicans blame the children for failure to meet unrealistic goals. In truth, Republicans know when they say things like that; the finger they're pointing at our kids is the middle-one.

> "Censorship reflects a society's lack of confidence in itself. It is a hallmark of an authoritarian regime."—*Supreme Court Justice Potter Stewart-1966.*

It's sad, but ignorance tries to now dominate our learning institutions. It's not the fault of the teachers, but by those charged to assure an adequate education is made.

In Colorado, a book that was being used as part of an English assignment was confiscated from freshmen at Norwood High School due to references of paganism and an alleged magnitude of profanity.

In 2005 at the one-horse town of Norwood, one parent sent a letter to Superintendent Bob Conder, according to Kathryn Heidelberg of the *Montrose Daily Press*, expressing concern over, *Bless Me, Ultima*, a book being used in the classroom as a literature book. Conder said the books, about 2 dozen in total costing $6.99 each, were pulled from the classroom, and designated to be destroyed. Upon hearing the "good news" the parent approached the superintendent and asked to burn the books instead of the school janitor destroying them.

Superintendent Bob Conder granted the parent the book-burning request. When asked Conder said, "I have not read the book." But, that matters little to zealots, "The point is, it contains language that everything else we do says is inappropriate," he said.

> "Where they have burned books, they will end in burning human beings."—*Heinrich Heine*, from his play Almansor (1821)

Thousands of books smolder in a huge bonfire as Germans give the Nazi salute during the wave of book-burnings that spread throughout Germany.

In Norwood, Colorado children are being told to be "good Nazi's" by a handful of misguided and ignorant people. Dare to understand different cultures, dare to learn "inappropriate" ideas and some level of retaliation is assured for the heresy.

The future of this country literally depends on how we invest in our children. While we spend trillions of dollars trying to think of new ways to kill other people, we are sacrificing the very future we presume to be preserving.

To defending this country is the highest form of sacrifice and the noblest of goals. However, there are far too many people interested in profit, not defense. These pirates have to justify their existence or else they have no means of profit.

One of the greatest fears of the Founding Fathers was the idea of a standing Army. They hated the idea, because they were observers of ancient Rome. If you have a standing Army, you will have war. An Army cannot exist in a world without war.

But, no one would dare suggest in today's world that we should to disband the military. So here we are, in a permanent state of war; in a war without end. We're shoveling trillions of dollars into an industrial complex that is seeing record profits, while our economy is hemorrhaging money; new and gruesome weapons are being developed to kill some hypothetical enemy while our kids are getting dumber by the day.

The United States military is 20 times more powerful than the next guy behind us, but we not dare think of shifting any of that to the home front to fight a war against ignorance.

Why?

Ignorance is far more profitable. If people were educated in what their leaders were doing, they would no longer be our leaders. Keeping our children ignorant is bliss to the Republican leadership.

Our security, the fate of the United States, is being wasted on those who really don't care about America, only themselves. Our schools should be the shrines of our society. Instead it's just a place to put our kids so they stay out of adult's way. Our tallest buildings, our greatest institutions, should be our schools; instead we worship at the altar of the Fortune 500. We stand in awe of the Sears tower, Trump tower and morn the death of the Trade Towers. We believe our success is measured by the amount of garbage we produce and how much we consume; lovingly called the Gross National Product. We spend billions every year on Gladiatorial games, which in the end produce nothing except what they're selling at half time. We worship the players of a hypothetical victory over another city, as "heroes" while our children, who worship us, are left to themselves on the weekends.

It's time we decide what's really important in this country.

What we do, will have some serious consequences for the very future of our democracy. The only question is, do you care?

Article 5 – Rebuild America, not just Iraq

Section (A): The Signatories are committed to protecting the right of every American to clean air, clean water and good, fertile soil . . . because the web of life depends on it.

Section (B): The Signatories shall defend America's right as Stewards of the planet, to protect her from irresponsible polluters and profiteers.

In the United States the number of Hunters and Fishermen has never been so low. This is in large part due to the Republican majority who give away our public lands to private industrial polluters.

These pollutocrats poison the streams where fish used to mate and feed. They fence off the water to wild-life who needs it to survive and wipe-out these same gaming animals as "vermin" because they dare to trespass on these public lands.

Sportsmen, who must ask special permission to hunt and fish on land they have a right to, don't dare actually eat what they catch for fear of taking in unknown toxic waste.

All across the country this problem has become pandemic in size. In Louisiana, the Jumbo-sized shrimp New Orleans is famous for are sporting dangerous levels of mercury. Pregnant women are warned not to eat the local seafood because it can now cause birth defects, like autism.

Check out the book, *Having Faith: An Ecologist's Journey to Motherhood* by Sandra Steingraber, a research Scientist of fetal toxicology at Cornell University. She writes about environmental threats to pregnancy and devotes two chapters to mercury.

Louisiana seafood is the second largest industry in that state, now in serious trouble by pollutocrats who dump toxic waste in our river-ways sending it down the Mississippi into the Gulf of Mexico. We're eating seafood being fished out of a giant toilet, then wonder why there are so many infant and Juvenal disorders.

What is the FDA & EPA's solution to this problem?

Don't tell the public. The scientific community is well aware the problem and has mountains of data to show the public, however, sycophants of pollutocrats like Majority Leader Tom DeLay, write legislation to prevent us from ever knowing about it. Republicans aren't just letting us eat and drink these toxic chemicals; they have business models that (in their minds) resolve the issue.

What is the solution to this problem by the Republican leadership?

"Free Trade"—we can always buy our seafood from the world's largest communist regime—China. Republicans believe by helping the Chinese economy decimate our mom & pop businesses, we are solving the problem of environmental destruction here in the United States. But, dare to point out that little fact and you risk being labeled "un-patriotic" by the Republican Majority.

Thanks to the "smart money" people in the Republican Party, the majority of Shrimp bought around the United States today, come from the shores off China's coast, a market once dominated by Louisiana. Now, we send our economic strength to communist countries rather than using that money to strengthen our own economy.

Why is this happening?

Republicans favor the industrial polluter because those industries fund their political campaigns. It would appear that the real definition of "patriotism" by Republicans is the security of their bank accounts, not the ideals or security of the United States.

A wise man once said that a person couldn't serve two Masters. The actual Master the Republicans Leadership serve espouses, "For the love of money is the root of all good." When it comes to serving the American people, where do you think you, (or your children), rank in the Republican Leadership food chain?

The answer to that question is surreal and macabre.

- **Industry rewrites government article on perchlorate dangers (12/19/04)**

A paid consultant for the industry-funded Perchlorate Study Group removed important information on the dangers of perchlorate from an article in the September 2002 issue of a government scientific journal, according to records obtained by Riverside, California's Press-Enterprise. The original story for the journal Environmental Health Perspectives contained information on Environmental Protection Agency studies showing how perchlorate, an ingredient in rocket fuel and a common groundwater contaminant, could cause brain damage in fetuses. The journal's editor allowed Gay Goodman, an industry consultant for the firm Intertox, to remove that information—along with a mention that the Perchlorate Study Group co-sponsored the EPA's research—from the article because it was "potentially very damaging" to the study group. The editor also approved re-titling the article as "Reprieve for Perchlorate: Effects Not a Significant Concern." These changes occurred without the author's knowledge or permission.

"My name was misused, and my journalistic reputation was misused," said Rebecca Renner, the story's original author. "It is outrageous that my article was changed by people working for industries that have a totally vested interest and a huge stake in the outcome of this issue, and that it was changed in a totally covert way."

The controversy has come to light as the National Academies of Sciences prepares to issue an independent review of perchlorate research next month—the result of which could lead to new perchlorate standards for drinking water. Industry has suggested that 200 parts per billion is a safe level of perchlorate for drinking water, however the EPA has recommended 1 to 6 parts per billion as a safe standard.

"Perchlorate contamination of drinking water threatens the health of unknown millions of Americans nationwide," said Erik Olson, senior attorney with NRDC's health program. "It's troubling when the industries responsible for this pollution hold more sway over our government's response than the concern for public health."

- **Outgoing EPA head approves increased use of cancer-causing pesticide (12/16/04)**

In violation of both an international treaty and the Clean Air Act, outgoing Environmental Protection Agency administrator Michael Leavitt signed off on new regulations allowing U.S. farmers who grow tomatoes, strawberries and other crops to continue using methyl bromide, an ozone-depleting and cancer-causing pesticide that had been scheduled to be phased out worldwide next year.

Methyl bromide was banned under the Montreal Protocol, a treaty signed by President Ronald Reagan in 1987 and supported by subsequent U.S. presidents from both the Democratic and Republican parties that is intended to protect the ozone layer. Methyl bromide has been shown to cause prostate cancer in agricultural workers and others who are directly exposed, according to the National Cancer Institute.

At a conference last month on the Montreal Protocol, the United States was among a dozen nations that successfully negotiated for continued "critical use" exemptions from the methyl bromide phase-out. The EPA exemptions will allow agribusiness interests to use 19.7 million pounds of methyl bromide next year, an increase of nearly 2 million pounds over the amount used in 2003. The EPA exemptions will also allow a handful of U.S. chemical companies to produce and import 17 million pounds of methyl bromide in 2005, even though they have already stockpiled more than 22 million pounds of the chemical. The rules violate conditions that countries use up the available stockpile of methyl bromide before authorizing new production—conditions the Bush administration agreed to in Montreal Protocol talks with 180 countries just last March.

"Catering to a handful of big chemical and agribusiness interests, the Bush administration is actually expanding the use of this dangerous, ozone-destroying chemical," said David Doniger, policy director of NRDC's climate center. "More methyl bromide means more ozone depletion and higher risks of skin cancer, cataracts and immune diseases for millions of Americans."

- **EPA ponders delaying Superfund listings and cleanups (12/02/04)**

Over the next 30 years, the Environmental Protection Agency estimates that 350,000 abandoned toxic sites will require federal cleanup—at a cost of up to $253 billion. But with the federal Superfund program strapped for cash and the Bush administration opposed to reinstating a "polluter pays" fee on industries to generate cleanup money, the agency favors a new approach to the problem: limit current funds to cleanup projects currently underway rather than listing new hazardous waste sites and allocating money for their cleanup.

"The suggestion that the EPA should ignore dangerously toxic areas and leave communities at risk from those contaminated sites, rather than force pollutocrats to pay for cleaning them up, is inexplicable, inexcusable and irresponsible," said Danielle Solomon, a Superfund expert who works for a coalition of environmental groups that includes NRDC. "Reinstating the 'polluter pays' fee and fully funding Superfund is the best and, really, the only way to address our nation's toxic cleanup needs," she added.

Quite plainly and literally, the Republican White House Administration and Republican leadership actions are killing us. They're killing us by choking us to death with poisoned air to breath. They're killing us with polluted water to drink. They're killing us by the pollution laced food we eat. And they're killing us with chemicals that create diseases of our own genetic code.

Many of these people don't care. The others are suckers for their own leadership propaganda. The true Leaders honestly believe their wealth will be there for them in heaven with streets paved with gold. That once they've trashed the planet, Jesus will come back and save them from themselves.

Article 6 – Healthcare for Americans not just Iraqis

Section (A): The Signatories respect all human life, without regard to race, religion, sex or sexual orientation.

Section (B): The Signatories will insure that approval or rejection of new drugs are based on real science and potential benefits, not politics and ideology.

We have said it before, the Republican majority is out of control and as of this writing George W. Bush has yet to veto a single spending bill. This is no surprise; its how he has bankrupted every business he has ever run. The "life, liberty and pursuit of happiness" of the United States is no different from any other Bush bankruptcy.

What is the result? We're in a healthcare crisis unlike any the United States has ever faced before.

We have six percent of the world's population and 50 percent of its wealth, yet we're the only industrialized country that doesn't provide at least basic healthcare for all its citizens.

Meanwhile, healthcare costs have more than doubled in the past 10 years, and health insurance premiums have doubled in just the past 5 years.

Even more outrageous, prescription drug costs in the past 10 years have increased 250 percent! (In one private pharmacy in Mission Viejo, California, the only one at the hospital, the market up is a minimum of 350%. How do we know this for a fact? My Campaign Manager stopped to purchase some medication there and refused the price having purchased the same medication in the same amount for less than 1/3 elsewhere. How much is the mark up at your favorite pharmacy?)

The Health Care Crisis didn't happen by accident, it's been engineered. Peter Rost, a vice president of marketing at Pfizer, points out that prices for patented drugs in 25 other top industrialized nations are 35% to 55% lower than in the United States. But, Rost says, the pharmaceutical companies do make exceptions here: "Our dirty little secret is that the drug industry already sells its products, right here in the U.S., at the same low prices charged in Canada and Europe. It's done through rebates."[2] Through such rebates the VA purchases a drug for $322 that elderly people who use the Republican Medicare discount card and have to pay $1,299 annually.

Rost cites a 2001 finding by Public Citizen that drug companies' favorite customers paid just a little over half the retail price. "This leaves the 67 million Americans without insurance to pay cash, with no rebates, at double the prices paid by the most-favored customers. The fight against re-importation of drugs is a fight to continue to charge our uninsured full price while giving everyone else a rebate." Rost says. It is a system which forces people, particularly the elderly, to choose between food and drugs. Rost cites a recent study of older adults with diabetes, one in three of whom said they went without food to pay for drugs. In the case of diabetes medically speaking, diet is a very important part of managing the disease, requiring less medication.

The sad part is that by requiring the uninsured to pay outrageous drug prices, they have less money for good diet and other preventative measures, thus shortening their lives and hurting families and loved ones while only benefiting Big Pharma!

The end result of this profiteering vice-hold by Big Pharma, the hospitals and insurance companies is a healthcare system in serious decline.

Even though 44 million Americans have no healthcare insurance, our inefficient hodgepodge of a healthcare system still manages to spend more per capita than any other nation, while overall health of Americans is rated just 37th in the world. We have shorter life expectancies and higher infant and child mortality than Canada, Japan and all of Western Europe except Portugal.

If GOP complacency for our children's safety was not true, why then would the Republicans in Congress demand the EPA relax rules to protect children from accidental exposure to rat poison? Could it be that the GOP received over $15 million dollars in contributions to put our children at risk?

Yes, it's true.

The EPA has received instructions from high-level Republicans to work with the Rodenticide Registrants Task Force (RRTF), an industry group designed to de-regulate rat poison.

Previously, pellet rat poison was required to have a bitter taste and have dark-dye to alert parents their children had gotten into something. After the change in the first two years alone, according to the American Association of Poison Control Centers (AAPCC), they reported nearly 60,000 cases nationwide of poisonings by Rodenticide between the years 2001-2003.

Now thanks to the "good Christians" the GOP who self-proclaims to be "pro-life" they leave parents in the dark on what happened to their children until the autopsy.

Apparently to some Republicans, the importance of "pro-life" in any given situation is directly proportional to the number of "dead presidents" they receive. The GOP has a strange idea on what "life" really means.

Article 7– Fairness: Media, Workplace, Elections

Section (A): The Signatories are committed to upholding the virtue of the Free Press over corporate ownership. The Signatories do defend every American's access to the power of the Press; giving voice to those often denied a voice.

Section (B): The Signatories recognize the need to keep America strong through its workforce, not the exporting of good jobs to slave-labor countries.

Section C: Voter-verified, auditable paper trails must be mandatory in every polling place in America.

4. Elections officials must be non-partisan.
5. Private companies may not run our elections through, proprietary, uninspected and unsecure software.
6. Voter suppression, intimidation and gerrymandering of electoral districts for pure partisan gain must stop forever.

Media outlets like the Fox news channel are out of control. They purport to the title of "news channel," however are little more than a propaganda department for Republicans exclusively. George W. Bush has even called other news outlets "unfriendly" because they refuse to hide information embarrassing to the sitting elite.

In an April 2004 White House meeting with British Prime Minister Tony Blair, President Bush proposed bombing the Arab TV network Al Jazeera's international headquarters in Qatar. On November 22, 2005 Britain's Daily Mirror published the shocking report that was based on a memo stamped "Top Secret" that had been leaked by a Cabinet official in Blair's government.

Why did Bush want to bomb a TV news network? Truth is very dangerous to tyranny, and George Bush knows which side of the truth he's on.

Democracy is based on the idea that we all have a voice in the way our government functions. A crucial element to a sound democracy is accurate information, or else we cannot make good choices on that government.

The portions of the media seem to have reached the point of criminal abuse on informing us what is factual and what is not. Some employ partisan political hacks to distribute disinformation, an action we don't tolerate in other countries, yet actively justify in this country. The information we need to take responsibility for our government has been denied to us by a 'Fox' in the hen-house.

In early January 2005 Tribune Media Services (TMS) terminated its contract with columnist Armstrong Williams after it was reported in USA Today he had accepted $240,000 from the Bush administration to promote the *No Child Left Behind* (NCLB) education-reform law on his TV and radio shows. E&P subsequently reported that Williams had also written about NCLB in his newspaper column at least four times last year.

In a statement, TMS said: "[A]ccepting compensation in any form from an entity that serves as a subject of his weekly newspaper columns creates, at the very least, the appearance of a conflict of interest. Under these circumstances, readers may well ask themselves if the views expressed in his columns are his own, or whether they have been purchased by a third party."[3]

Rep. George Miller, D-Calif., ranking Democrat on the House education committee, said the Williams contract "is propaganda, it's unethical, it's dangerous and it's illegal. ... This is worthy of Pravda." Committee Chairman John Boehner, R-Ohio, agreed to join Miller in requesting an inspector general's investigation.

On January 9, 2005 at the *Republican Roundtable*, Al Hunt suggested there are more Bush employees masquerading as journalists. "I'm sorry, Armstrong. Listen, I'll tell you this. I'll bet that there will be a great market for FOIR, Freedom of Information Requests, in the next couple weeks because I suspect Armstrong Williams is not alone. There have been other people who've been doing this."

There are several investigations about fake news produced by the Bush administration, actions that constituted illegal "covert propaganda," according to an investigation by the Government Accountability Office (GAO).

In one Bush propaganda video, titled "Urging Parents to Get the Facts Straight on Teen Marijuana Use," news stations were provided a script for the news anchor. It reads: "Despite the fact that marijuana is the most widely used illicit drug among today's youth, many parents admit they're still not taking the drug seriously. Now the nation's drug experts in health, education and safety have joined the drug czar to speak directly to parents about the serious risks of teen marijuana use. Mike Morris has more."

After interview snippets with "drug czar" John Walters, who heads the drug-control policy office, and other experts, the story closes with the voiceover: "This is Mike Morris reporting."

Television stations knew the materials were produced by the Office of National Drug Control Policy, nothing in the two-minute, prepackaged reports would indicate to viewers that they came from the government or that Mike Morris, a former journalist posing as a "breaking story," was working under contract for the government.

"You think you are getting a news story, but what you are getting is a paid announcement," said Susan Poling, managing associate general counsel at GAO. "What is objectionable about these is the fact the viewer has no idea their tax dollars are being used to write and produce this video segment."[4]

What we are witnessing today is the result of Ronald Reagan's 1987 abolishment of the Fairness Doctrine, which had required media to report both sides on controversial issues.

Today that requirement is gone, and <u>many media outlets report only the news that benefits them directly. Media will report on new "miracle</u>

drugs" that not coincidentally, the parent news company owns substantial shares in, or will promote a film being released by the parent company as though it was newsworthy.

The FCC itself has clearly said "rigging or slanting the news is a most heinous act against the public interest and indeed, there is no act more harmful to the public's ability to handle its affairs."

The FCC has yet to punish anyone (besides those who consider themselves Democrat) presumably because the head of the FCC is a Bush appointee.

- **Media Pornography**

The Washington Post's Terry Neal recently wrote about the shell game the media plays on all of us. "...corporate leaders at companies as diverse as News Corp., Marriott International and Time Warner can profit by selling red-state consumers the very material that red-state culture is supposed to despise. Those elites then funnel the proceeds to the GOP, which in turn has used the money to successfully convince red-state voters that the other political party is solely responsible for the decline of the civilization."

Neal cites two court cases involving so-called pornographic films— in Utah and Ohio—that have revealed in two of the "reddest" areas in America, the "community standards" included a huge consumption of porn, even among Mormons.

Timothy Egan, in an earlier piece for The New York Times, wrote, "The General Motors Corporation, the world's largest company, now sells more graphic sex films every year than Larry Flynt, owner of the Hustler Empire. The 8.7 million Americans who subscribe to DirecTV, a General Motors subsidiary, buy nearly $200 million a year in pay-per-view sex films from satellite providers." Also, Rupert Murdoch—owner of Fox News and an ardent pro-Bush conservative—"makes more money selling graphic adult films through its satellite subsidiary [Echo Star] than Playboy, the oldest and best-known company in the sex business, does with its magazine, cable and Internet businesses combined."

AT&T, once the nation's largest communications company, offers a hardcore sex channel [Hot Network] and owns a company that offers sex videos to a million hotel rooms in America. One in five of AT&T's customers pay $10 a film to see "real, live all-American sex—not simulated by actors." AT&T is (big surprise) one of the largest donors to the Republican Party.

Enter Jeff Gannon an online reporter for Talon-News.com and often given a White House Press "Day Pass." Gannon, (whose real name is Jim Guckert), tossed propaganda questions to Bush while respected journalists were sent to the back of the bus.

Gannon contemptuously asked Bush in January 2005 at a news conference how he could work with Democrats "who seem to have divorced themselves from reality."

And somehow, Gannon was also given a classified CIA memo by someone in the White House that named agent Valerie Plame, leading to his grilling by the grand jury investigating her outing. It was later revealed, in July 2005, by Matt Cooper's emails subpoenaed from Time Magazine, the White House leak came from Gannon's buddy Karl Rove.

Gannon left his post in the White House Press Corp a few months prior to Rove's naming as the source.

However, the issues of national security for information on outing our agents, or getting access to the White House on a daily basis under a false name were not the reason Gannon quit his cushy White House position.

Gannon was ousted for his alleged involvement into creating an online male prostitution ring, including male porn sites *HotMilitaryStud.com*, *MilitaryEscorts.com* and *MilitaryEscortsM4M.com*.

"The issue here is whether someone with connections to male prostitution was given unfettered access to the White House and copies of internal CIA documents. For a family values administration, that's pretty creepy," said John Aravosis, the original Blogger chasing the story.

After it became public, the Bush administration's boy-toy abruptly quit the "news" organization. Quickly thereafter, all of the stories Gannon wrote were erased from the *Talon-News.com* web site. A great many were on gay issues, including one detailing John Kerry's "pro-homosexual platform" that was headlined mockingly, "Kerry Could Become First Gay President."

The corporate media, with the integrity to make a big deal out of the "inaccurate" report by CBS' Dan Rather about President (AWOL) Bush, now had another opportunity to weed-out those who make the media look bad. However, when it came to Jeff Gannon, CNN's Wolf Blitzer came to Gannon's rescue.

On his show, Blitzer spoke with Howard Kurtz of CNN's "RELIABLE SOURCES" and "The Washington Post" interviewed Kurtz from "The Washington Post newsroom."

Blitzer asked, "Is there any evidence that there's a connection, that the White House put him up to this to throw these kind of questions whether to Scott McClellan or to the president? Any evidence of wrongdoing, first of all, on the part of the White House?"

"No evidence whatsoever," Kurtz quickly responded. "I talked to Scott McClellan about this today, the White House spokesman. He said, first of all, President Bush didn't know who Jeff Gannon was when he called on him at that news conference."

There you have it. The White House denied any involvement, so the case is closed. No reason to do any further investigation into the matter. Pay no attention to the naked-gay-conservative-male-prostitute sitting in the middle of the gay-bashing Family Values® White House living room, nothing here to see.

That's a very strange position for a reporter to take. A responsible question could be asked: Why don't Blitzer and Kurtz ask the obvious questions?

Feeling the pressure from the Internet, where the Gannon-Gate story first surfaced, the media is starting to take notice they are being out-scooped and shamed by people with real day jobs. This army of renegade journalists called web-loggers or "Bloggers," has sent a chill up the spine of the cookie-cutter media jet-set.

Kurtz added, "It's fine to disagree with [Gannon's] politics, but did [Bloggers] go too far, I think a lot of people are asking, in dragging in some of this personal stuff?"

What an odd position to take, one might even suspect Kurtz was doing a little bait-and-switch for his buddies in the White House. Was it going too far dragging in the "personal stuff" of a male prostitution ring from a guy who self-proclaims "good Christian values" and being a born-again Christian? Was exposing such hypocrisy going too far when said "journalist" had no qualms in manufacturing like-minded rumors about John Kerry and others?

And, it's worth noting that prior to the *illegal* invasion of Iraq by George W. Bush, Scott Ritter, a former UN Weapons Inspector, had his personal and professional life destroyed by the same Press Corp for publicly saying the pretext for "Weapons of Mass Destruction" was a lie. The Bush administration leaked Ritter's background of an arrest in a misdemeanor charge he was later exonerated from, but the so-called "liberal" media used it to discredit the messenger, who it turns out was absolutely correct.

A few days prior to the Gannon-Gate scandal, the Manchurian-beefcake knew Bloggers were looking into his background and taunted them to try and find anything. Saying "I'm hiding in plain sight," Gannon wrote an essay daring them to find out his secret identity. When they did, he ran to Blitzer crying foul and disingenuously proclaimed he was a victim of liberal terrorists.

> WOLF BLITZER: Because one of the things, as you know, that were said is that you had some sexually explicit Web sites that you were working on. I don't understand what that is, but maybe you could explain that.
>
> JEFF GANNON: Well, several years ago, before I came to Washington, I had registered various domain names for a private client. I was doing Web site development. Those sites were never hosted. There's—nothing ever went up on them. And the client went on to do something else. - CNN, 2/10/05

Any novice police interrogator could deduce through Gannon's facial ticks and eye movements, he was being "less than truthful" on CNN. It was discovered within hours that observation was, in fact, correct.

One particular website called *AmeriBlog.com* and written by John Aravosis, found that in 1999, Paul Leddy, a Web designer and photographer, received an email from a man named "Jeff" from Wilmington, Delaware. Jeff wanted Paul to build him a new Web site for his business. Paul accepted the job, provided Jeff mailed him a check with half the money up front (Jeff had not provided a last name, and Paul wanted to make sure he was for real). Jeff sent the check, it cleared, and Paul built the site and launched it online for Jeff.3

Paul pulled from his archives pictures (above) of "Jeff" and compared them to the images of Gannon (below).

Paul didn't think about Jeff much until he heard about a breaking scandal involving a man named Jeff who owned several military escort service Web addresses. "I saw the name Jeff Gannon, knew our Jeff, saw the militarystud.com Web address, and thought 'hmmm, everything was military that sounds like Jeff who we did the site for.'"

Paul searched the Internet *WhoIs* director for *militarystud.com* and saw that the owner was Bedrock Corp of Wilmington, Delaware. "That's definitely him," Paul said. (Paul and a second source both recall Jeff paying with a check in the name of Bedrock Corp. The name stuck in their heads at the time because they asked Jeff why "Bedrock"? He replied something about the Flintstones, they recall.) This is relevant because Bedrock Corp in Wilmington, Delaware also owns former White House reporter Jeff Gannon's personal Web site and a series of Web addresses apparently dealing with military male escorts.

Paul then went and checked his files. He found five invoices to Jeff from August 31, 1999 to March 30, 2000. (The file properties say Paul Leddy created them on those dates.)

Metaphorically in a fashion of Romulus and Remus, Jeff sought refuge by quickly running to the warm and nurturing teat of the Wolf.

During his plea for victim status on CNN's Wolf Blitzer, the journalist formally known as Gannon, even went so far as to say he and his family were being stalked by vigilante liberals while on their way to church. However, the real facts show these threats could not have happened when they did. His real identity was not made public until Monday night at

11:54pm February 7, 2005 only three days before his interview with CNN. No church services were going during that time period. Blitzer nevertheless simply took Gannon's explanations as fact and never questioned his rhetoric, despite Gannon's bankrupt credibility.

Howard Kurtz of "RELIABLE SOURCES" needs some perspective in what constitutes going "too far." If the Bloggers suddenly find a blue dress stained with genetic material, then he has a right to ask the question did Bloggers "go too far." Until then, Kurtz only shows his true colors by journalistic malfeasance.

This is just more proof (as if any more were needed) the media is anything but "impartial." Anyone who believes differently is the victim of right-wing mythology.

Imagine the media explosion if a male escort had been discovered operating as a correspondent in the Clinton White House. Imagine that he was paid by an outfit owned by Arkansas Democrats and had been trained in journalism by James Carville. Imagine that this gentleman had been cultivated and called upon by Mike McCurry or Joe Lockhart—or by President Clinton himself. Imagine that this "journalist" had smeared a Republican Presidential candidate and had previously claimed access to classified documents in a national-security scandal.[5]

Republicans might have mounted another Civil War with like-minded "Freedom Fighters" such as the terrorist group *Operation Rescue* to bomb federal buildings or activated terrorist cells like the *Branch Davidians*.

In a letter to President Bush, Rep. Louise Slaughter, a Democrat, questioned why the Manchurian Beefcake routinely received credentials for White House news briefings. "It appears that 'Mr. Gannon's' presence in the White House press corps was merely as a tool of propaganda for your administration," Slaughter wrote.

The White House had no comment.

The Sun newspaper of Baltimore, Maryland ran an open letter questioning "how a partisan political organization and an individual with no credentials as a reporter—and apparently operating under an assumed name—landed a coveted spot in the White House press corps."

The question has merit. Many legitimate news organizations, including the *New Hampshire Gazette*, are denied White House access by the Bush administration, despite the Gazette being the country's oldest newspaper and one of the original publishers of Thomas Paine's *Common Sense* before the Revolutionary War.

However, the Bush administration has proven that patriotism is defined as those who support the destruction of democratic values.

The White House Press Secretary Scott McClellan said neither he, nor the White House has any say in who gets access into the Press Room. In these times of heightened security, the official White House stance is highly unlikely, if not outright laughable.

The Bush administration since day one has controlled every aspect of the news media. A fact confirmed by many long-time journalists. Even Maureen Dowd of the New York Times, from the famed "paper of record" has felt the cold hand of engineered White House news.

"I was rejected for a White House press pass at the start of the Bush administration," Dowd said in a February 17, 2005 Op-Ed in the New York Times. "But someone with an alias, a tax evasion problem and Internet pictures where he posed like the 'Barberini Faun' is credentialed to cover a White House that won a second term by mining homophobia and preaching family values?"

It is quite disturbing a political hack from a fly-by-night website who allegedly refused to give his real name to national security officers at the White House, was given free reign. The fact that this so-called "journalist" also created male porn/prostitution Internet sites only adds to the ghastly hypocrisy of the Family Values® Republican cult.

While it is un-proven whether Gannon took any money from the government for his boy-toy services in the Press Corp, it has not been ruled out either as we see the Bush propaganda machine starting to break down.

Syndicated columnist Maggie Gallagher has also apologized to her readers for not disclosing a $21,500 contract with the Department of Health and Human Services to help create materials used to promote Bush's $300 million initiative encouraging straight marriage to strengthen families.

HHS later disclosed that a third conservative columnist, Mike McManus, had received $10,000 to promote Bush's marriage initiative, according to an Associated Press report. His weekly column appears in about 50 newspapers.

"It is a brilliant strategy," wrote Frank Rich in the New York Times. "When the Bush administration isn't using taxpayers' money to buy its own fake news, it does everything it can to shut out and pillory real reporters who might tell Americans what is happening in what is, at least in theory, their own government. Paul Farhi of *The Washington Post* discovered that even at an inaugural ball he was assigned a 'minder' - attractive women who wouldn't give him their full names - to let the revelers know that Big Brother was watching should they be tempted to say anything remotely off message."

A Pentagon Office of Strategic Influence, intended to provide propagandistic news items, some of them possibly false, to foreign news media was shut down in 2002 when it became an embarrassing political liability. But much more quietly, another Pentagon propaganda arm, the *Pentagon Channel*, has recently been added as a free channel for American viewers of the Dish Network.

These "new ideas" by the Republican leadership are, in fact, fairly "retro," dating back to 1930's Germany. What's sad is Republican propaganda blueprint has been lifted right out of *Mien Kampf* (My Struggle)-chapter six-*War Propaganda* by Adolf Hitler.

> "The function of propaganda does not lie in the scientific training of the individual, but in calling the masses' attention to certain facts, processes, necessities, etc., whose significance is thus for the first time placed within their field of vision.
>
> The whole art consists in doing this so skillfully that everyone will be convinced that the fact is real, the process necessary, the necessity correct, etc. But since

> propaganda is not and cannot be the necessity in itself, since its function, like the poster, consists in attracting the attention of the crowd, and not in educating those who are already educated or who are striving after education and knowledge, its effect for the most part must be aimed at the emotions and only to a very limited degree at the so-called intellect.
>
> All propaganda must be popular and its intellectual level must be adjusted to the most limited intelligence among those it is addressed to. Consequently, the greater the mass it is intended to reach, the lower its purely intellectual level will have to be. But if, as in propaganda for sticking out a war, the aim is to influence a whole people, we must avoid excessive intellectual demands on our public, and too much caution cannot be exerted in this direction."
> – *Adolf Hitler*

The Bush administration, knowingly or unknowingly, followed Hitler's advice with the utmost precision. When it came to justifying the Iraqi invasion, it was all about "Weapons of Mass Destruction" because Paul Wolfowitz said it was the easiest point for the public to consume. Did the Republicans believe WMD's were in Iraq? Probably, but fear of the use of WMD's by Iraq was reserved for the general public alone.

The Media was more than willing to promote these frauds by the White House, not because they had no evidence to the contrary, but in spite of evidence to the contrary.

Every news organization has been intimidated, and reporters who have done stories the administration finds embarrassing have received threats about their careers. The administration has its own quasi-official state TV network in *Fox News*; hundreds of rightwing radio shows, conservative newspapers and journals and Internet sites coordinate with the Republican apparatus.

This is wrong! We own the airwaves and the media has a responsibility to uphold, by telling us the Truth. The media exist because the American people allow them to exist, not the other way around. The corporate media has been negligent and we must now fix the problem.

The sycophant Party says the media is "liberal." Could there be a bigger lie?

Do you really think ideologically charged Republicans, who own the media would hire liberals or would allow liberalism to thrive on their news networks? Do you think ideological Republicans, who own the advertisements, would promote their products on liberal news networks?

Yet these news networks exist and there is nothing impartial about them, just as there is nothing impartial in propaganda itself.

The Fairness Doctrine needs to be reinstituted to bring the roguery of media outlets like Fox News under control, **even if it requires a Constitutional Amendment**. In truth, media abuse is at the very heart of our now dysfunctional democracy, even putting our national security in serious jeopardy.

Enter Robert Novak, the syndicated columnist, CNN talk-show host who apparently loves outing our CIA agents, putting their lives and the lives of their informants in danger abroad.

It is a federal crime to reveal the name of Valerie Plame, a CIA undercover agent. Yet as of this writing, Novak, nicknamed the "Prince of Darkness," by his colleague's walks free and has yet to stand before a judge.

Why?

Outing the agent served the political purposes (political revenge) of the White House for said agent's spouse not worshiping President Bush's official faith-based religion; that the belief Weapons of Mass Destruction were being built in Iraq. It is a practice of character assassination that seems to have been repeated over and over again, as it was with the former UN Weapons Inspector Scott Ritter.

It is true that you can take the matter of Fox News' abuse into your own hands by purchasing a channel blocker like those made for porn. If you go to Foxblocker.com and order their little device for $8.95, not only can you prevent yourself from exposure to the ignorance and brutality of Sean Hannity or Ann Coulter, Foxblocker.com will also send Fox News an email telling them they lost another potential viewer forever.

While the satisfaction of ordering this device is instantly gratifying, it does not resolve the issue. The entire media has sacrificed its own ethics in-lieu of greed and profiteering, corrupting a pillar our democracy for selfish ambition. And, since the media is unable to police itself, it is our responsibility to bring them back into sobriety.

In part, this is already happening. The Internet has been tremendously successful in bring news outlets back to reality, specifically the Blogs. There have been several cases where Blogs have forced the media to address issues of their own integrity when they say things not founded in fact, or without any facts. In one case, a Broward County businessman had touched off a firestorm of controversy with an Internet report that the news chief of CNN accused American troops in Iraq of deliberately killing journalists.

Rony Abovitz, co-founder of the Hollywood medical technology company Z-Kat Inc. ran from his Blog an account of remarks he heard from Eason Jordan, CNN's chief news executive. The panel discussion at an economic conference in Switzerland not only rocketed around the Internet, but triggered fierce attacks on CNN from mainstream media critics.

"When thinking people, especially journalism professionals, say something like that—that U.S. troops might be war criminals—and can't substantiate it, you've got to follow it up," said Jack Shafer, media critic for the influential website *slate.com*. "Blogs always seem to ask much tougher questions of a powerful media figure than Time magazine or The New York Times or Newsweek do."

During a Jan. 26, 2005 panel discussion of threats to reporters, Abovitz was shocked to hear CNN's Jordan say American troops in Iraq had "targeted" journalists and killed a dozen of them.

"He was going on and on about it," recalled Abovitz. 'My first thought was, gee, have I been missing something? And I stood up and asked, 'Is this documented? And if so, why hasn't it been on the cover of Time magazine? Because if it's true, it's much bigger than [U.S. military abuses at] the Abu Ghraib prison.'"

According to Abovitz, Jordan seemed surprised at the question. "He kind of froze, and then he started backpedaling. But the crowd included a lot of people from the Middle East, who were cheering him on, so then he wiggled back and forth.'

'When Abovitz posted his original account of the panel, more than 400 other Blogs took up the battle cry. These Blogs pressured the mainstream news organizations into covering the story.

That finally happened with stories in the Washington Post, the Boston Globe and other papers, as well as on CNN's rival cable news networks.

Media critic Shafer from *Slate.com* said the utter enormity of the Blog response forced the story onto newspaper front pages. "What they were practicing was virtuous pack journalism," he said. "Everybody thinks pack journalism is bad, but sometimes, like on 9/11, you want a pack. This was pack journalism at its best."

This marks the second time in a short few months that Blogs have surfaced a major controversy over television news. Blogs were the first to accuse CBS' 60 Minutes of using forged documents in a story last year on President Bush's Vietnam-era National Guard service.

Their claims eventually forced CBS to retract the story and launch an internal investigation that cost Dan Rather his anchor job and resulted in the dismissal of five other CBS staffers.

CNN chief news executive Eason Jordan quit a few days after the story went "mainstream" amidst a furor over the remarks he made in Switzerland.

Abovitz, for one, is impressed. "This is a new era where you can't just make statements anymore. There are too many eyes. The Blogs are like a million little cameras and tape recorders."

The Republican majority has started to take notice of this behavior and Bloggers are realizing what they say is a double-edged sword.

According to an article in the *Christian Science Monitor*, one writer suffering from "pure boredom" working as a features writer for a North Carolina newspaper was sacked for the sin of keeping a Blog. Rachel Mosteller began keeping an online journal, anonymously, with names changed to protect the guilty. She chronicled the people who inhabit just about any newsroom - the foul-mouthed female reporter, the chubby sportswriter, the co-worker who hoards the free books sent in by publishers seeking reviews.

However, her blog, called the *Sarcastic Journalist*, didn't stay secret for long. Her bosses found out, and Ms. Mosteller, eight months pregnant at the time, was promptly shown the door.

She learned a valuable lesson: If you have a job, blog at your own risk - "unless you're writing recipes and about how much you love puppies and kittens," Ms. Mosteller says.

The fact this happened in an institution that self-proclaims a right to the First Amendment, yet denied it to others is very disturbing. In fact, when it comes to your constitutional protections, your employer doesn't care, nor are they obligated to care. If you dare to write something that is perceived as "unflattering" by your employer in any way, you're toast. People all over the country have learned that simple fact the hard way.

The idea that a whistle-blower can expose the ugliness from within an organization sends cold shivers down the spin of the corrupt. This extends to what your personal politics are, or what religion you may believe. If your employer doesn't approve of your point of view, it's the unemployment office for you.

Thus, getting private citizens fired from their employers for daring to question GOP methods is the perfect backlash coming from the Republican camp. Reagan weakened the Unions, and under relentless attack by the Republican machine, this disregard for American values has become commonplace.

- Jeremy Zawodny was fired from the search engine company *Google.com* for his Blog.

- Michael Hanscom, fired in October 2003 as a temp at *Microsoft* for posting a picture of Apple Macintosh G5s sitting on the loading dock at MS. Troutgirl, fired from Friendster for blogs that included references to her work.
- Matthew Brown, fired from *Starbuck's* for posting comments about the coffee chain, its customers and managers on his personal blog in September 2004.
- Penny Cholmondeley, terminated from her post as *Nunavut* (Canada) Tourism marketing officer after someone anonymously complained about her blog to her employer, which included passing references to the locale.
- Iain Murray, a Brit working in the US, fired from his post as Director of Research at an *NPO* in January 2003, apparently in part due to blogging at work.
- Steve Olafson, fired from his job reporting for the champion of the First Amendment the *Houston Chronicle* after another reporter outed him as the anonymous force behind a blog that was critical of local politicians and other news sources.
- Daniel P. Finney, also fired from a job as a reporter, but at the *St. Louis Post-Dispatch,* another warrior for Free Speech, they discovered he was blogging, in part about his news assignments.
- Jessica Cutler (*Washingtonienne*) fired in the summer of 2004 after blogging for a total of two weeks about her sexual exploits with six partners, including a few highly placed government staffers.
- Heather B. Armstrong, whose experiences as an outed blogger first to her Mormon family, and later to her employer, helped coin the term "dooced." She was fired in February 2002.
- Amy Norah Burch, who was fired from her job as undergraduate coordinator for the Committee on Degrees in Social Studies at *Harvard University*, after "a handful of unflattering references

to her workplace interspersed throughout the site's archives raised eyebrows at the department." May 2004.

We own our government; it should be bound to our will. But we cannot make intelligent, principled stands without the benefit of accurate, impartial information from a free . . . and fair and balanced press. We must put an end to the abuse of our media by those in power.

Article 8 – Right to take-home pay

Section (A): In the first 100 days of regaining the Majority in Congress, The Signatories will consistently act to close the deficit and balance the budget by reversing the tax cuts of the Bush Administration for those that make over $500,000.

Section (B): Regain surplus to pay down debt as soon as possible.

Every child born in 2005 will have to pay a proverbial "Birth Tax" of $36,000 to pay down the current deficit, courtesy of the Republican Majority of the last six years. While Republicans try to completely eliminate the Inheritance Tax, a fee that affects only the wealthiest 2 percent of Americans, by renaming calling it a "Death Tax," EVERY baby born will have to face the Republicans' "Birth Tax." It is not a tax literally due and payable as few American families can pay it, but it is the acknowledged reality of the tax cut and spending spree of the Republican controlled House and Senate for the last six years.

Because we can't just vote to repeal our debts!

The late Senator Everett McKinley Dirksen once said during a budget debate, "A million here, a million there, pretty soon you're talking serious money."

Of course today we routinely talk in "billions," while Republicans glibly assure us that deficits don't matter.

What they mean, of course, is that deficits don't matter to them. Why?

Today we are a debt driven society and the old morals of debt being a form of slavery have gone the way of the founding fathers. In the America of the Republican leadership its ok for everyone to act like a silver-spooned college freshman with their very first credit card.

Unfortunately, this is the downside of a psyche that has trained itself to look at quarterly profits rather than the long-term health of the organization and its people. Everything is short term and myopic. If the business goes bust, who cares? Just pillage the assets and put them under a new corporate name.

In this case, however, it's the future of the United States and our people that's at stake, not some paper entity that can be created and destroyed as easily as one would change their underwear.

Flouting fiscal responsibility, our leaders have borrowed hundreds of billions from nations as far from our ideals as Saudi Arabia and Communist China, as if these tyrannical regimes have America's best interests at heart. The result is TRILLIONS of dollars of debt, giving other nations the power to bring us crashing down without firing a shot -- by merely calling in our debt!

So deficits DO matter, and even more to our kids and grandkids than to us, because they're the ones who'll have to pay for the short sighted and gluttonous behavior of today's Republican controlled House and Senate. The sins of the father are indeed passed on to the nation's sons and daughters.

Like that silver-spooned college freshman, Republicans seem to believe that someone else should pay for their partying. It doesn't matter if it's Mommy, Daddy or someone else's children, as long as they get what they want now!

Well in every sense, the time has come for their "party" to be over! Our children's future is at stake.

- The nation's infrastructure is crumbling...power blackouts in New York and Los Angeles reveal neglect and vulnerability; New Orleans failed levy system brought us devastation that will cost $200 billion to rebuild from while it could have been fixed for **one percent** of that.

- The "No Child Left Behind" law is an under funded sham, substituting standardized tests that pit poor schools against rich schools and take time, effort and money from more meaningful education. In other words, teachers are being told how and what to teach, by clueless politicians.
- Meanwhile, because of the NCLB under funding, states and local school districts are required to make up the difference through tax increases.
- Rather than improving school facilities and teacher pay and education, the GOP's other solution is vouchers, which would leave the poorest schools and the students most in need, in worse shape than ever.
- At the other end of the education spectrum, cuts are being made in college student grants and loans at a time when college costs are skyrocketing due to cuts in grants and funding to the colleges!
- This Republican education agenda may ultimately be the basis for a government-sanctioned, cradle-to-grave, economically divided society.
- By cutting funds for Head Start and other pre-school programs, this Congress further signals that they don't really care about even the most vulnerable of our nation's children.

Every time a Republican decides to spend billions on pet projects when we have a deficit of hundreds of billions, he's voting to raise taxes on our children.

Every time a Republican votes to give tax money back to the wealthiest Americans, he's voting to raise taxes on our children.

Every time a Republican votes for subsidies for Fortune 500 companies, he's raising taxes on our children.

Every time a Republican votes to outsource our jobs overseas to help American companies be "more competitive," he's raising taxes on our children . . . and making them less likely to be able to pay those taxes!

And as long as this deficit exists, every time a politician votes to raise his own pay, as Congress has built in on an annual basis, he's voting to raise taxes on our children.

Article 9 – Representation Not Domination

Section (A): The Signatories are committed to upholding the virtue of the United States Democracy.

Section (B): The Signatories shall defend America's Democracy from all forms of attack, foreign **and** domestic, including the greatest threat to her existence since the beginning of time, the illegitimate authority of theocracy.

> "One of the biggest changes in politics in my lifetime is that the delusional is no longer marginal. It has come in from the fringe, to sit in the seat of power in the Oval Office and in Congress," says Bill Moyers. "For the first time in our history, ideology and theology hold a monopoly of power in Washington."

The Religious Right has reduced their argument for changing the United States from a Democracy to a Theocracy with a singular bumper-sticker philosophy of "America is a Christian Nation." They say that was the "intent" of the Founding Fathers. But, what did the Founding Fathers really have to say about it?

> "The clergy believe that any portion of power confided to me [as President] will be exerted in opposition to their schemes. And they believe rightly: for I have sworn upon the altar of God, eternal hostility against every form of tyranny over the mind of man."—*Thomas Jefferson* to Benjamin Rush, 1800

It's sad the issue on whether or not the United States should be a theocracy even need to be an issue. One would think this is a no-brainer. Yet it's the argument put forth by an army of televangelists who seek riches and glory for themselves walking hand in hand with Republican sycophants who swore upon the bible to uphold the Constitution, not the other way around.

The Republican leadership has realized that 82 percent of Americans consider themselves religious, but according to the Christian pollster Barna Research, only 4% actually hold the same worldview as the Religious Right. That's roughly the same margin of the homosexual population. The difference is the latter remain a consistent while the numbers in the Religious Right are crashing. That translates into less tithing, less political power, and even more frightening to the Religious Right, insecurity and doubt that they may be, in fact, wrong.

The real reason for this drive for theocratic control of our government is a smoke-screen for an agenda of bigotry. As illegitimate as theocracies are in government, they are the only form of government that endorses and encourages bigotry. It is no coincidence that the biggest advocates of theocracy also happen to be the world's biggest bigots, who hide behind the bible to justify their malfunction, like cowards.

> "The feminist agenda is not about equal rights for women. It is about a socialist, anti-family political movement that encourages women to leave their husbands, kill their children, practice witchcraft, destroy capitalism, and become lesbians."—*Rev. Pat Robertson*, fundraising letter, 1992
>
> —
>
> "I really believe that the Pagans, and the abortionists, and the feminists, and the gays and lesbians who are actively trying to make that an alternative lifestyle, the ACLU,

> People for the American Way, all of them who have tried to secularize America. I point the finger in their face and say 'you helped this to happen.'"–*Rev. Jerry Falwell* (After Sept.11th, 2001 while the Trade Towers still burned)
>
> [...]
>
> "I totally concur!" –*Pat Robertson* (Speaking with Falwell)

So strong is the hatred these bigots have for anyone outside of their own, they would disregard all the sacrifices made by so many people, paid for in blood, so they can hate anyone and everyone freely.

> And we're going to invite PETA [to "Wild Game Night"] as our special guest, P-E-T-A—People for the Ethical Treatment of Animals. We want you to come; we're going to give you a top seat there, so you can sit there and suffer. This is one of my special groups, another one's the ACLU, another is the NOW—the National Order of Witches [sic]. We've got—I've got a lot of special groups. –*Rev. Jerry Falwell* (November 21, 2004 televised service, broadcast from his Thomas Road Baptist Church)

Televangelists like these are, arguably, one of the biggest threats to the United States and Christianity itself, in either history—more so than Communism, or even Nazism from WWII. Journalist Seymour Hersh has said "We've Been Taken Over by a Cult" while speaking at Stephen Wise Free Synagogue in New York in 2005. Hersh is a Pulitzer prize-winning investigative journalist who first exposed the Abu Ghraib torture scandal in the New Yorker magazine in April 2004 and is author of *Chain of Command: The Road From 9/11 to Abu Ghraib.*

This cult is willfully trying to overthrow our democracy through a coup d tat of lies and deceit.

> "A nation can survive its fools, and even the ambitious. But it cannot survive treason from within. An enemy at the gates is less formidable, for he is known and carries his banners openly. But the traitor moves among those within the gate freely, his sly whispers rustling through all the galleys, heard in the very hall of government itself...He rots the soul of a nation . . . he works secretly and unknown in the night to undermine the pillars of a nation. . .he infects the body politic so that it can no longer resist. A murderer is less to be feared."—*Cicero*, the great Roman orator, 42 B.C.

In the bigoted minds of the Religious Right a rationalization is made of pro-slavery for everyone "lower" than they are, in which they also decide who is and who isn't "lower" by having the authority to say who is/isn't sufficiently "Christian enough" for their liking. Not so ironically, in their minds the color of one's skin is a strong indication of Christian ranking.

> "The Republican Party of Texas reaffirms the United States of America is a Christian Nation ..."—*State of Texas GOP Platform, 2002*

This is why these televangelists consider democracy a pagan ideology; why they lie when they blather about the Founding Father's "intent" was a "Christian Nation." These televangelists hate democracy for daring to say, "All men are created equal," and believe democracy is a Jeffersonian error.

> "All persons shall have full and free liberty of religious opinion; nor shall any be compelled to frequent or maintain any religious institution" –*Thomas Jefferson*

Don't believe it?

> "Washington isn't the problem — democracy is."— *Patrick E. Kennon*, The Twilight of Democracy[6]

Still not convinced?

> God has graciously granted America—though she doesn't deserve it—a reprieve from the agenda of paganism. Put your agenda on the front burner and let it boil. You owe the liberals nothing. They despise you because they despise your Christ."—*Bob Jones III President of the openly racist Bob Jones University to George W. Bush after the stolen election of 2004*

Surely these "men of God" believing in keeping the United States... united?

> "There can be no unity between Christianity and other religions listed, because they do not believe that Jesus Christ is 'the truth' and the only way to be reconciled with God."—*Pat Robertson*[7]

Well, so much for the Religious Right's faux "*Judeo*-Christian" lip-service. The true colors of such political correctness are simply a mask to placate the masses. The respect the Religious Right has for its so-called co-religionists is clear. Bob Jones III has also said that Islam, Judaism, and

Roman Catholicism are "a false religious system." Bob Jones also claims, "the Bible itself is intolerant and true followers of God's word should be as well."

Bob Jones III is a very influential leader within the Religious Right and the Republican leadership and is working hard every day to accomplish his vision of the world.

Do you want to see how the Religious Right respects our Constitution? Here the Religious Right is speaking of the two most prominent Constitutional watchdog organizations from the November 22, 2004 edition of FOX News Channel's Hannity & Colmes:

> FALWELL: Up until this generation with the influence of the American Civil Liberties Union and anti-Christ groups like Americans United for Separation of Church and State -
> COLMES: Oh "anti," that's not true, Reverend. They're not "anti-Christ."
> FALWELL: It is true. I know those guys and the fact is they're so anti-religious, anti-Christian that they have tried to secularize the country.

What the Religious Right doesn't like to admit, "Secular" was real intent of the Founding Fathers. Don't believe it? Let's look it up.

The American Heritage Dictionary defines "secularize" as:

> sec·u·lar·ize   *n.* 1) To transfer from ecclesiastical or religious to civil or lay use or ownership.

So in Falwell's mind, 'How dare the Founding Fathers suggest a*verage people* own the United States, and not the Church...that's Paganism!' In fact, that's what the Religious Right says every time they blather, "America is a Christian Nation." The Founding Fathers knew it is impossible to have a "Free Country" and an official state religion.

> "The clergy, by getting themselves established by law and engrafted into the machine of government, have been a very formidable engine against the civil and religious rights of man."—*Thomas Jefferson to Jeremiah Moor, 1800.*

The time has long since past that those elected officials who believe in the United States; believe in her Constitution, and work to protect her from tyranny, also standup and have the stones to exclude the politics of bigotry who exclude everyone else. It's time to call a spade a spade and tell bigots to be-gone. As Americans we have a right to be the Bouncer and eject a handful of unruly people who can't play nice with others.

It is true, Bigots have a First Amendment right to exclude those people they don't want in their institution, (Christian Legal Society, Boy Scouts, Military, etc...) but Enlightened institutions also have a First Amendment right to exclude Bigots.

Though they wail and whine about it, Bigots can't have it both ways.

The First Amendment is a wonderful idea. People have the right to choose the Religion of their liking, but they also have the right to exclude those religions they don't agree with. We have the Freedom of Religion *and* The Freedom from Religion, at the very same time.

We have the right to say "I don't agree with your religion because it acts like, 'If the Money Changers can't go to the temple, then bring the temple to the Money Changers.'"

An argument that is hardly exaggerated when one considers the Starbucks in a kiosk at Grace Capital Church in Pembroke, N.H. Or, at True Bethel Baptist Church in Buffalo, N.Y., the spot where the choir once sang now sells Subway sandwiches. And in more than a few charming houses worship all across the country, hymns and prayers ascend through a steeple that doubles as a leased-out cell phone tower.[8]

One would think in the Religious Right's Bible, the Sermon on the Mount starts off by saying, "Blessed are the *rich* in spirit[9]...Blessed are the *warmongers*: for they shall be called the children of God"[10]

Remember James Watt, President Ronald Reagan's first secretary of the interior? Watt told the U.S. Congress that protecting natural resources was unimportant in light of the imminent return of Jesus Christ. In public testimony he said, "After the last tree is felled, Christ will come back."

In truth, when the Religious Right acts that way and claim it's biblically sound, they're not lying. It is biblically sound to the one written by Anton Szandor Lavey,[11] just not Peter, Paul, Luke and Mark.

This too is perfectly legal.

The Religious Right has every right to believe what they want. They can be greedy, bigoted, self-righteous, indignant and contemptuous. However, opposition to their imposition is not victimization. The Religious Right cannot force themselves upon you or your children without your permission, regardless of how much they arrogantly cry and falsely complain victimhood.

That is the virtue of a Democracy. You have rights, and exercising those rights does not mean the system is broken.

In a Theocracy you don't have that choice. You and your children must follow the god (or emissaries thereof) of whoever happens to be in power and there are always groups who seek to hold that power solely for them. If you dare use your own brain to discern truth from imposture, to follow the guidance within your heart, you risk a gruesome death of your whole family. Why? Your truth threatens the corporal power of a small group of men consumed with a blood lust.

The Middle East is a perfect example of theocracies at work. There are super-poor and uber-wealthy with no middle-class while corruption and tyranny are the standard. Most people there can never hope for anything better than to look out the hole, (they would call a window), in their mud-baked asylum, hoping death will better than the state of misery they were born into. Thanks to the ruling Theocracy, it's created a standard of living in which being a suicide bomber starts to look pretty darn good.

If the Religious Right have their way, that is the future of America. They can only see riches and glory for themselves, dreaming of the day they can smite those who dare to think for themselves or refuse to believe their dogma.

> "World conquest…It is dominion we are after. Not just a voice… not just influence…not just equal time. It is dominion we are after."—*George Grant, high ranking Religious Right leader.*

It is true, the Religious Right can never be accused of having an original thought, as the idea is hardly new. This theocratic hijacking of the world's strongest super-power happened to the Roman Empire when Constantine was ruler. Thus bringing to an end the greatest Republic in the world and plunging the planet into darkness for almost two thousand years. That is until the Found Fathers established the United States of America, creating the standard now admired throughout the globe. It is quite certain, even the Founding Fathers could never have imagined what their actions had upon the world.

The Religious Right is quite upset about it too. If only they had been born a little over two centuries ago, they might have been able to stop the pagan ideology of Democratic governess in its heathen tracks. Such was the opinion of the Official Church of England, the Anglican Church, over two hundred years ago. No matter, at least this way the Religious Right can use modern tools to more easily control the masses while the whole world comes to lick their nuclear-tipped-boot-straps.

The *followers* of the Religious Right believe their rise to power is blowback for losing the civil war and having to free the slaves. In truth, they live in the land of pink fluffy bunnies and unicorns, justifying bigotry in their minds. The reality is far more sinister.

The formula for the Religious Right's rise to power is not a new idea either. It was a well-disciplined structure following the advice of the 15th century drunkard Niccolo Machiavelli, the same formula used by Machiavelli's infamous pupil, Adolf Hitler.

> "Democracy, the deceitful theory that the Jew would insinuate. Namely that all men are created equal." -- *Adolf Hitler*, "Mein Kampf," In Politics/Nazism

Sound familiar?

> "If the positive element of Christianity is love of one's neighbor, that is, caring for the sick, clothing the poor, feeding the hungry and quenching the thirst of the parched, then we are true Christians!" –*Adolf Hitler*[12]

The Religious Right would most certainly be upset over the comparison. They would not however, be upset the comparison *can* be made, or else they would stop using Hitler's political playbook.

The Religious Right would say, 'That's outrageous! We would never do what Hitler did!'

> "No one...has hitherto been persecuted for his religious views, nor will any one be persecuted on that account!" –*Adolf Hitler*[13]
>
> "The Anti-Christ is alive in our time, and is a male Jew"—*Jerry Falwell*,[14] Thursday, January 14, 1999
>
> "God Almighty does not hear the prayer of a Jew."— *Bailey Smith*, (a founding father of Robertson's Christian Coalition)[15]

Can you hear the Religious Right saying 'Wanna buy a bridge? There's a beautiful one in San Francisco, no really...*trust me.*'

In fact, the top bananas in the Religious Right promote the belief Hitler tried to remove God and religion from government. This is in error; Hitler loved the Christian religion and incorporated as much "God speak" as he could get his hands on. It was Hitler that declared Germany a "Christian Nation" and unified all Christianity under the Evangelical Church of Germany. The Vatican under Pope Pius XII agreed with much of Hitler's distaste for democracy and sought position in what looked like a new thousand year era for Europe. Yet in our time, Supreme Court Justice Antonin Scalia has tried to tell Jews they are "safer" in a Christian Nation.[16]

In the same light, discussing the American Civil Liberties Union's (ACLU) objections to the Dover, Pennsylvania, school district's plans to include "intelligent design" theory in their high school biology curriculum, FOX News host Bill O'Reilly declared on January 19, 2005: "Hitler would be a card-carrying ACLU member. So would Stalin. Castro probably is. And so would Mao Zedong."

In the dysfunctional minds of Religious Right, defending our Constitution and democracy is *both* Communist and Fascist, despite the polarizing opposition to each other. The error is clear, as well as the Religious Right's malfunction in believing those who exercise their rights, prove the system is broken.

O'Reilly has previously labeled the ACLU a "fascist organization" and "the most dangerous organization in the United States of America right now ... second next to Al Qaeda."

When dealing with pathetic shells of human character, like Bill O'Reilly whose perversity is obvious (by a simple *Google* search with the word "loofah.") It is not necessary however, to wallow in the depths perversity to correct the error. We own this country and they are little more than opportunists trying to insight discontent for self-pontification.

Dr. Joseph Goebbels, the Nazi regime's Propaganda Minister, directed the campaign that enthused mundane Germans to action against Jews, asked "Are the German people going to be sitting ducks all over the world for Jew murderers?" the radio voice challenged by the Rush Limbaugh of the 1930's. "Are the German people to stand helpless while the Fuhrer's representatives are shot down by the Jew swine? Are the Schweinehunde to get off scot-free? Is the wrath of the German People against the Israelite scum to be restrained any longer?" Goebbels blathered.

Today, right wing Christian fundamentalists are claiming things even more ridiculous by saying that Christmas—and therefore Christians—are under attack. They vowed that they were not going to take it any more and are organizing terrorist cells (militia) to inflict some "Godly justice."

Don't believe it? Do a Google search under "Freeper" (Free Republic) and be careful not to soil yourself.

Just because they're greedy, envious, hateful, bigoted and vengeful—does that make the Religious Right evil?

Not really, it just means they're filled with greed, envy, hate, bigotry and revenge, other than that, they're pretty nice people. Even though the Religious Right walks around like their waiting for a vacancy in the Trinity, they are plainly incompetent to lead anyone into a bakery, let alone lead the most powerful country in the world.

This too, they cannot do without your permission.

As of this writing, Republicans are cramming through Congress the so-called *Streamlined Procedures Act of 2005*, a bill that makes it close to impossible for wrongly convicted people to prove their innocents through DNA evidence.

The blood lust of executing innocent human life for crimes they didn't commit seems to be the cherry on top of the Republican mandate. This is "Compassionate Conservatism" in action, folks. And, for all the whoopla about letting Terri Schiavo die "is murder," from *Focus on the Family*, (a Republican theocratic cult), when innocent people are slated for execution by the state, *Focus and the Family* is mute.

Why? It's blood lust, plain and simple. Not so coincidently, a large percentage of those wrongly convicted also happened to have darker skin than the whites-only Party in Washington.

It is true that Republican sycophants have taken control of our government and are actively pursuing the agenda of the Religious Right. By no means do all of Republicans agree with the Religious Right, just the GOP Majority. But, you have the power to take our government back and hold Republicans accountable (despite their attempts to dodge accountability) even if that involves prison time for conspiracy against the United States...it is all up to you.

Our system of justice does not wait for criminals to change their ways, nor do our courts allow criminals to police themselves. It is the citizenry that decides innocence or guilt and for that reason alone, politicians are frightened.

Scott Ritter a former senior UN weapons inspector in Iraq between 1991 and 1998 and is the author of *Frontier Justice: Weapons of Mass Destruction* and the *Bushwhacking of America* who argued against the Bush administrations justification of *Weapons of Mass Destruction*, prior to the *illegal* war in Iraq has said, "The invasion of Iraq was a crime of gigantic proportions, for which politicians, the media and the public share responsibility. If history has taught us anything, it is that it will condemn both the individuals and respective societies who not only perpetrated the crime, but also remained blind and mute while it was being committed."[17]

The difference between politicians/media and the general public is the public bares the burden of generational guilt, while the politicians/media bare the burden of increased quarterly profits, without shame or remorse. To the Religious Right and the Republican Party, this is a win-win situation.

The Signatories shall, however, defend the United States from those who would destroy her democracy. Do struggle in moving forward into the 21st century with the hope of a better world. Not just for a select group of pseudo-religious bullies, but better for everyone to create a stronger America and a healthier humanity.

Just like the rules on a play-ground, standing up to bullies takes courage, but it's the right thing to do and indeed, it's the only option left.

Through our democracy we have engineered our current way of life. We have produced the best minds in history. We have inspired entire cultures to reject their kings, their dictators and their emperors. Our democracy has redeemed humanity from thousands of years of cruelty and ignorance, opening eyes from a myopic form of bondage that most believed could never be freed.

The only catch is our democracy leaves us responsible for our decisions, whether we like it or not. Freedom isn't free. We are responsible for those we elect because they represent our desires. If that equates to tyranny, we cannot complain because we did it to ourselves. The virtue of America, however, is that every two years we have the opportunity to over-throw the government.

Could there be a better time than now?

In a democracy masochism is perfectly legal. But, is that the way for the leader of the free world to behave? And bare in mind, when a democracy enters into the perversity of bondage, it ceases to be a democracy.

The only question is: Who would you support, Thomas Jefferson, or Rev. Pat Robertson?

"Pluralism is the name given to the transition period from one orthodoxy to another.... Every other great nation has unified around some ethical standard. Lack of unity is a sign of ultimate destruction." –*Rev. Pat Robertson*

—

"Is uniformity attainable? Millions of innocent men, women, and children, since the introduction of Christianity, have been burnt, tortured, fined, imprisoned; yet we have not advanced one inch towards uniformity. What has been the effect of coercion? To make one half the world fools and the other half hypocrites. To support roguery and error all over the earth." -*Thomas Jefferson*, "Notes on the State of Virginia" [1781-1785]

Pat Robertson has called Thomas Jefferson a "red-headed liberal." It would appear that what Robertson means as "liberal" is anyone willing to defend our Founding Fathers *real* intent.

A lot of Christians would say, 'Pat Robertson doesn't speak for all Christians.'

You don't get much higher on the Religious Right's food chain than Rev. Pat Robertson. And, the Religious Right is deciding through Republican sycophants what is religious and what is not, despite its theology, or whether the Religious Right itself, is biblically sound. Whatever Rev. Pat Robertson says is "Christian" so shall it be—by law.

The only way for the true Americans of Christianity to speak for themselves is to throw out the GOP Majority. Anything less is to just sit back and accept Rev. Pat Robertson as your new American Pope, with all the bondage that comes with it.

However, as the poet Dana Tidwell once said, "Never confuse an open mind with one that is merely vacant." If you honestly believe that Rev. Pat Robertson is your Messiah, you've got bigger issues than could ever be resolved from a book…and good luck with that.

To the remaining 96% of the United States, the day has arrived when we tell the Religious Right, in a singular and reverberating voice, "America is a Democracy! If you don't like it, go to the Middle-East, but stop trying to over-throw my country…or else."

Most politicians lack the stones to confront the Religious Right because they don't want to be accused of persecuting Christians, a noble frame of thought, to be sure. However the Religious Right has set the standard. Just because someone self-proclaims to *be* a Christian does not mean they truly *are* Christian.

> "You say you're supposed to be nice to the Episcopalians and the Presbyterians and the Methodists, and this and that and the other thing. Nonsense! I don't have to be nice to the spirit of the Antichrist."—*Pat Robertson.*[18]

What's wrong with using their-own rule of measurement on Christian authenticity? They could hardly complain about that, (wink, wink).

In truth, the politics of bigotry cuts both ways and the Religious Right is neither. Those who believe that "All men are created equal" need to recognize the Religious Right gets its authority, not from God or the Bible, but from us, and we're going to take it back.

Do you know what you call a tyrant without followers?

Lunatic.

They know without us, they are just mad-men screaming into the desert. The Religious Right fears beyond anything else that their world-view will be proven wrong. Their only hope is that we are asleep at the switch.

Their dread is now our plan, because we know enlightenment is not to be feared.

> "We hold these truths to be self evident: that all men are created equal; that they are endowed by their Creator with certain unalienable rights; that among these are life, liberty, and the pursuit of happiness." - *Thomas Jefferson*

Democracy, not Theocracy, is our Founding Father's intent. That's the way they designed it, that's the way it will be again...by any means necessary.

Article 10 – We Live Up To Our Promises

Section (A): The Signatories vow to uphold to the Democratic tradition of helping Americans from all corners of society to realize the American Dream.

Section (B): We pledge to inspire the dreams of all living Americans.

Once was a day when America was strong, and not divided by the war against the middle class. Parents and grandparents gave their children savings bonds for birthdays and holidays, to help build America while helping to provide for college or later life needs.

Thanks to the Republican majority, that day is no longer an everyday reality.

No one likes to pay taxes, least of all the super rich! So the argument has been made that average Americans will be better off financially if the wealthiest Americans are allowed to keep more of their money.

That is a lie.

Since Republicans have come to power, the government has swelled in size beyond any point in its history. This costs money; lots of money.

Many Republicans are even sickened by what their leaders have done to this country.

Representatives of the Heritage Foundation, a conservative think tank, write, "Public diplomacy has been weak, and sound foreign policy initiatives have failed to win support from our allies (in Iraq) because they were not accompanied by well-planned public diplomacy efforts. Observers can therefore be forgiven for concluding that

> Bill Clinton's declaration that 'the era of big government is over', now seems rather premature."

It's hard to find a parent who says they've given up on their children, or on America, but with Republicans in control; it sometimes seems that American Government Leadership has given up on us.

If you vote for politicians who allow the wealthy, who should pay for government because they reap the greatest benefits, to dodge their responsibility, then you and your children are paying the difference. And the chances that you will ever achieve wealth are greatly diminished.

This is the agenda of the "ownership society."

The myth of trickle-down economics that today's Republicans have adopted was correctly called "Voodoo Economics" by George H. W. Bush. The wealthiest don't feed the economy; they feed off the economy!

They invest in overseas businesses, stash in offshore accounts and horde natural resources as their own, pretending it's their right as "patriotic Americans" or even worse, claiming it's what Jesus would do!

Why, for example, gut the bankruptcy law? This is a law specifically designed to protect those who most need it; the people with overwhelming debt and few or no resources for repayment. Greed, pure and simple of the companies that can keep their own assets from being 'written off' is the only reason.

And this "banker's dream" is becoming a reality through the support of Republicans who've decided, as they often do with social issues, to pick and choose when to follow biblical teachings.

Greed is a defect, not a virtue. But to today's Republican leaders the concept spoken by JFK, "Ask not what your country can do for you, ask what you can do for your country," is seen as heresy to the "greed is good" agenda.

What does the God who many Republican Leaders claim to worship have to say about all of this?

> "Wealthy cheaters will not be spoken of as generous, outstanding men. Everyone will recognize an evil man when he sees him and hypocrites will fool no one at all. Their lies about God and their cheating of the hungry will be plain for all to see. The smooth tricks of evil men will be exposed, as will all the lies they use to oppress the poor in the courts." --Isaiah 32: 5-6

Apparently God has distaste for greed as well.

Nevertheless, thanks to media outlets like Fox News, the CEO's of the world have convinced the average American voter their interests are the same.

Yet 25 years ago, the average CEO made 42 times more than the average worker; today they make 431 times as much!

Consider Enron and its former CEO, Ken Lay.

As of this writing, the golden boy of corporate malfeasance has yet to answer a single question on how his Fortune 100 Company was able to perpetrate one of the largest frauds in history. Does his friendship with the man he helped put in the White House have anything to do with this?

And who paid for this fraud? We did -- the taxpayers and the shareholders -- and $50 billion later, Ken Lay still walks free with millions in the bank.

Consider the invasion of Iraq.

First you thought we were invading because of weapons of mass destruction. Wrong! Indeed, if you thought we invaded because of any serious treat to the United States, you were watching too much Fox News and listening to too much "conservative" talk radio.

In April 2005 a Presidential Commission determined the pretext for invasion of Iraq, WMD, was dead wrong and cited this as a "major intelligence failure."

It seems hard to believe that 60 percent of those who get most of their information from Fox News and talk radio still believe Saddam Hussein was responsible for 9/11. But polls consistently show that they do.

The reality is that we invaded Iraq because the oil industry, in which Bush and Cheney were deeply involved, got tired of hunting for oil in unknown regions of the world. Instead they chose to steal the world's second largest oil supply. Problems arose, however, when Iraqis decided that they, in fact, owned their oil, not multi-national corporate barons.

Realizing too late that Iraq was a more "unknown" region than they'd thought, Republicans were aghast at these Iraqi rebels. Who, they considered, do these Iraqis think they are holding our oil hostage under their land!

The time has long passed that we get tough on "street crime," starting with Wall Street!

The bank-robbing bandits of the Old West are alive and well, but they're not hiding in shacks in the desert. They walk the halls of power, unbridled and unchecked. And they've shifted huge amounts of the nation's wealth into their own pockets, leaving the rest of us twisting in the wind.

Consider the 2004 Christmas season. Stores like Wal-Mart had expected 3 to 4 percent sales growth after Thanksgiving; what they saw was a 3 percent decline. K-Mart sales dropped 10 percent.

Meanwhile, high-end retailers like Nieman-marcus and Tiffany's are thriving, illustrating the huge gap between "haves" and "have-nots."

> "You have wealthy consumers spending in unprecedented proportions while cash and credit starved consumers are suffering" says retail analyst Burt Fleckinger of the Strategic Resource Group.

Why are lower income consumers suffering? Gas prices and home heating costs are up more than 30 percent from a year ago, taking an extra $1 billion from American's pocketbooks *every week*. Consumers are feeling the pinch trying to get a handle on just paying their own credit cards and increased rates on their homes.

This means less or nothing for savings, less or nothing for shopping and a much lower chance of ever attaining any level that might be described as financial wealth.

Good thing Republicans were honest when they said their $600 tax breaks would benefit Joe Thousandaire -- Not! The day when these buccaneers of the business world can take food out of the mouths of our children and retirement security from our grandmothers must come to an end -- Today!

While it's true that CEO deadbeats own the Republican majority, *you and I still own America . . . and it's time we remind them of it!*

The time has come for CEO deadbeats to be held responsible for their actions. But while Republicans say CEO's can police themselves, the reality is quite different. Both Republicans and the CEO deadbeats work hard every day to assure they'll never be held accountable, never be caught and have to pay for putting their hand in the cookie jar.

But it's clearly a direct conflict of interest to trust many CEO's to do the right thing; that's why they had to buy the GOP and turn it into the party of sycophants.

It doesn't have to be this way. As Americans we have the right to choose who represents us.

Corporations don't have this right, yet they seem to be in control. It's as if our Founding Fathers' idea for a free country has been sold off to the highest bidder and Republicans are eager to broker the deal with international corporations who have no loyalty to God or country.

Our national ideals not only suffer for this, but our economy suffers as well. The U.S. bond market overseas is "sluggish" (Wall Street jargon for "nonexistent") and to resolve that issue Republicans encourage corporations to "outsource" our jobs overseas to sweatshops and slave labor.

Some foreign investors also say they don't buy our bonds because of our foreign policies.

And when you think about it, why would investors abroad want to help the United States finance the possible invasion of their own country by corporate mercenaries, armed by our military? Would you have invested in Nazi Germany's bond market (Prescott Bush notwithstanding)?

Sadly, that's how much of the world sees the U.S. today, largely due to the foreign policy of our Republican leaders. There seems no greater tragedy than for America to be viewed as the very evil we'd spent over 200 years and millions of lives to fight against.

Are we doomed to be thus humiliated? Today's Republican Leadership, it seems, have been unintentionally or intentionally (depending on your view) orchestrating our fall from virtue -- from the noble enterprise of democracy, even as they claim to want to "spread Democracy!"

When 80 percent of the world sees us as the greatest threat to world peace, it's not out of envy or hating our freedoms. It's because Republican Leadership has a view of the world that doesn't work doesn't seem to care about anyone but themselves.

Domestically as well, the current leadership seems to have deliberately sabotaged the value of our currency. The U.S. Treasury defaulted on contracts with investors, mostly individuals, who loaned the government money in 1979 on agreement they would receive 9.125 percent interest every year until their bonds mature in 2009.

But the Bureau of Public Debt called for the redemption of $4.6 billion in 30-year bonds issued May 15, 1979, on May 15, 2004, five years before promised.

Bondholders of course were not forced to cash them in immediately, but they will not receive any further interest as had been promised.

The Treasury Department claims these bonds were called in to reduce the cost of debt financing and will result in the government saving $544 million. But that's the approximate amount our national debt increases about every six hours! So the excuse is clearly fraudulent.

> Gasp! The Bush administration lied to us again? Who would have thought?

The U.S. has started defaulting on our bond notes because Republicans either don't see the danger of corrupting our Triple A bond rating . . . or they don't care.

Thanks to Republican Leadership, no longer can politicians and bureaucrats brag that the United States has never failed to live up to its reputation as the safest investment in the world. Investment is no longer guaranteed by our word, and indeed, we're less credible than Sadaam Hussein in some parts of the world. This is not hyperbole; our image in parts of the world really is this bad!

As a result, the overseas bond market for the U.S. has tanked, the dollar is slouching toward nothingness against the Euro, and international corporations are raking in record profits by destabilizing American currency.

Meanwhile Republican leaders admonish us to "Stay the course" . . . on the road to oblivion.

The so-called "Smart Money" people in the Republican camp have turned the House of Representatives into a burlesque house where ethics are danced around like a brass pole, while corporate criminals walk free, war crimes are committed in our name, theocrats chip away at our democracy and apocalyptic utopians flirt with the big nuke 'em button.

What does this mean for you and me? Higher Taxes . . . or taxes by any other name -- user fees, "revenue enhancements" . . . if we're lucky! The burden is on our shoulders, and the future of our children and grandchildren.

Because when this out of control Congress tells us we're getting tax cuts, pay attention to the details. More than 80 percent of those cuts go to the wealthiest 10 percent of the population.

Did you make $7 million last year? No? . . . then you hardly qualify as important enough for these Republicans to care.

Republicans know they can't do this without our permission. But rather than be honest about it, they've lied or negated our authority by working loopholes for their corporate benefactors. Every time they do this, the future of our children and grandchildren . . . and the fate of our nation . . . are further left hanging in the balance.

These right wing extremists seem to think we are fools when they self-proclaim Christian "family values." They know the master they serve is neither Christian nor Biblical.

Acting as if "the love of money is the root of all good," these sycophants in government commit acts in our name to destroy our families and our livelihood. They actually believe we won't notice, won't see the error of their ways or question their shtick.

• Corporate Rights

Did you know that paper entities have more rights under corporate law than you do? Did you know that your Constitutional rights and even Our Creator are trumped by copyright laws?

In 1999 the "seed police" at Monsanto Corp. snared soy farmer Homan McFarling and the company demanded he pay hundreds of thousands of dollars for alleged technology piracy. McFarling's sin? He saved seed from one harvest and replanted it the following season, a revered and ancient agricultural practice.

Farmers have sought that wisdom in the Bible as "teaching a man to fish." But to the new Gods in mega-corporations, they may as well own the copyright on "fish," and you must buy the rights to feed your family. And don't keep any leftovers! You must throw them away and buy the rights all over again next season.

The "evil" of saving Monsanto seeds, genetically engineered to kill bugs and resist weed sprays, violates provisions of the company's cumbersome contracts with farmers and endangers its stranglehold over creation!

Since 1997 Monsanto has filed similar suits 90 times in 25 states against 147 farmers and 39 agriculture companies according to a report by The Center for Food Safety, a biotechnology watchdog.

In some cases copyright laws have literally destroyed farmers. In Tennessee, farmer Ken Ralph was sued by Monsanto and sentenced to

The New American Compact

eight months in prison after he was caught hiding a truckload of cotton seed for a friend.

His prison term was the first resulting from a criminal prosecution by Monsanto but a landslide of others is expected in the next decade. Ralph was also ordered to pay Monsanto more than $1.7 million.

If the situation was reversed and farmers were suing Monsanto, the President of the United States would be giving speeches about the cost of "frivolous lawsuits!" But since corporations have no soul to save nor body to incarcerate, it's not likely the roles could ever be reversed.

And that's really the point.

More examples: The U.S. Supreme Court in 1980 allowed the patenting of genetically engineered life forms and exclusively extended the same protections to altered plants in 2001. In 2005 a federal appeals court specifically upheld Monsanto's copyright on plant life.

Did you know, under the Gnome Project (mapping human genetic code); corporations actually hold the copyright on YOUR genetic code? God may have created us, but the patent is held by Monsanto and Dow Chemical.

This is like someone owning the copyright on the snowflake and billing ski resorts for the privilege of fresh powder! Sadly, in Republican land, that day may not be far in the future!

Let's contrast what happened in the early 1900's with what copyright law is doing now. Gandhi led India's people to the shores of their country to mine salt, believing it was their right, by God, as a natural resource of their country. But England held a monopoly on all the salt purified in their colonies.

All non-English salt was considered contraband, like opium or heroin, and Indians were forced to buy their salt from the British despite having an abundance of their own.

What's the difference between those same contraband laws and what is now happening to our farmers through copyright laws? Very little if you believe we have certain God-given rights.

Unfortunately, multi-national corporations don't believe in people's God-given rights. Trade agreements like NAFTA and, CAFTA, are nothing more than legalized slavery of other countries by multi-national corporations, directly hurting Americans financially and morally.

Under CAFTA, if a company is required by U.S. law or court order to clean up environmental damage, or even under EPA laws to create cleaner gasoline, they can sue the United States for billions for "loss of revenue." For anything that hinders their "inalienable right" to make a profit, these companies can legally sue all of us for billions of dollars.

Environmental laws, protected lands, nature preserves . . . they're now open to corporate pillaging . . . or lawsuits.

Though the government may not be able to do these things, Republican leaders have enabled CEO deadbeats to have considerable power over these Constitutional freedoms, "endowed by our Creator."

They only want government big enough to act as the enforcer of corporate law against us -- their contracts, their copyrights and their "intellectual property."

To them, profit is a right, risk is too darn risky and the basic laws of supply and demand are for wonks.

Privacy advocates note that a committee recently set up to advise the Homeland Security Department on privacy issues is so filled with Republican lobbyists that it amounts to the fox guarding the henhouse.

One member of the committee works for a high-tech company that distributed software accused of containing spyware.

Another member works for a conglomerate whose subsidiary turned over personal records of airline passengers to a government contractor.

A third works for a defense contractor from which thieves stole personal information on thousands of employees, exposing them to possible identity theft.

Bruce Schneier, chief technology officer of Counterpane Internet Security, a Mountain View, CA, computer security company, and author of "Beyond Fear," said he looked at the 20-member list and laughed. "It's just plain weird," Schneier said.

"Where are all the privacy people?"

Why worry about privacy when they can make a profit from our personal information . . . as though we were *their* property!

Personal privacy was so important to our Founding Fathers they ingrained it in the Constitution. But such ideas no longer seem important to government today, largely due to corporate profiteers, not fear of terrorism, as many Republicans in Congress claim.

Meanwhile, making these companies pay their fair share is downplayed political campaigns as "unnecessary regulation" that "hurts business." And we make up the difference!

When a company seems to have gotten too far out of hand, and someone sues, the victim is vilified for filing "frivolous lawsuits" . . . that "hurt business."

Yet these sometimes-huge awards given through lawsuits are the only things keeping some CEO deadbeats honest. The government doesn't protect us anymore, and multi-national corporations never did! So if we can't sue these robber barons when they are guilty of gross misconduct, they have nothing to fear from us, ever!

But don't you see? That's the point!

George W. Bush put it this way. "I'll work with Congress to reform asbestos litigation. (Applause). Asbestos lawsuits in Southern Illinois and elsewhere have led to the bankruptcy of dozens of companies, and cost tens of thousands of jobs. Many asbestos claims are filed on behalf of people who are not sick. The volume of asbestos lawsuits is beyond the capacity of our courts to handle, and it is growing. More than 100,000 new asbestos claims were filed last year alone. Congress has begun considering options to improve the current system for handling asbestos lawsuits. They need to act and get the job done. I look forward to signing an asbestos reform in 2005."

Never mind that the effects of cancer-causing asbestos have been generational since its use began in the early 1900's. One could even call it pandemic in causing cancer, but to the self-proclaimed "compassionate" Republicans, this is the granddaddy of "frivolous lawsuits."

What ever happened to the idea that this is the "United" States of America?

Shouldn't we be working toward a common goal for the betterment of this country? Shouldn't we be trying to spread the idea of freedom through our example instead of tyranny through the greed of a handful of men? What good is it to own the whole world if we loose our soul in the process?

The Founders created the United States of America as the last great hope for humanity. In the two hundred years since this bright light of freedom has existed, it has become the standard in which all countries have tried to achieve.

Yet, at the peak of this noble experiment called America, she has lost her way to the petty and tyrannical ambitions of a small cabal who really despise the idea of democracy itself. We have become victims of pride, pretension, arrogance and envy, because marketing has told us that we should be. We have allowed others to think for us, because we trusted them with the American dream. They only thing we didn't understand is they only wanted it for themselves.

It's time *We, the People*, turn things around and send charlatans and frauds packing. And while we're at it, take our pound of flesh from the hide of those responsible for stealing our nation's wealth. They have no say in the matter, but we do.

And for that reason, they are frightened.

The Democratic Party has a long tradition of helping America at times when America needs good leadership the most.

When the corporate greed of the 1920's culminated from the predatory nature of the nations wealthiest into the Great Depression, the Democrat Franklin D. Roosevelt stood up to the plate. What FDR did was define what the soul of America was by making government take care of the people. In the Preamble of the Constitution, that's the job of our government by caring for the "general welfare." FDR solidified that with his "New Deal," and Republicans are quite upset about it too.

To this day, Republicans and Fortune 100 companies have tried with some amazing success to gut, suspending and neutering what FDR did 80 years ago.

PROGRAM:	DESCRIPTION:
Emergency Banking Act/ Federal Deposit Insurance Corporation (FDIC)	On March 6, 1933 he shut down all of the banks in the nation and forced Congress to pass the Emergency Banking Act, which gave the government the opportunity to inspect the health of all banks. The Federal Deposit Insurance Corporation (FDIC) was formed by Congress to insure deposits up to $5000.
Federal Emergency Relief Administration (FERA)	Led by Harry Hopkins, a former social worker, this agency sent funds to depleting local relief agencies. Within two hours, $5 million were given out. Mr. Hopkins believed that men should be put to work and not be given charity. His program also funded public work programs.
Civil Works Administration (CWA)	This public work program gave the unemployed jobs building or repairing roads, parks, airports, etc.
Civilian Conservation Corps (CCC)	This environmental program put 2.5 million unmarried men to work maintaining and restoring forests, beaches, and parks. Workers earned only $1 a day but received free board and job training. From 1934 to 1937, this program funded similar programs for 8,500 women.

Indian Reorganization Act of 1934	This act ended the sale of tribal lands and restored ownership of unallocated lands to Native American groups.
National Industrial Recovery Act (NIRA) of June 1933	The decline in the industrial prices in 1930s caused business failures and unemployment. The NIRA was formed in order to boost the declining prices, helping businesses and workers. The NIRA also allowed trade associations in many industries to write codes regulating wages, working conditions, production, and prices. It also set a minimum wage.
Public Works Association (PWA)	The PWA launched projects such as the Grand Coulee Dam on the Columbia River.
Federal Securities Act of May 1993/ Securities and Exchange Commission (SEC)	This act required full disclosure of information on stocks being sold. The SEC regulated the stock market. Congress also gave the Federal Reserve Board the power to regulate the purchase of stock on margin.
Tennessee Valley Authority (TVA) (May 1993)	The TVA helped farmers and created jobs in one of America s least modernized areas.
Works Progress Administration (WPA) 1935-1943	This agency provided work for 8 million Americans. The WPA constructed or repaired schools, hospitals, airfields, etc.

Farm Security Administration (FSA)	The FSA loaned more than $1 billion to farmers and set up camps for migrant workers.
National Labor Relations Act (Wagner Act)	It legalized practices allowed only unevenly in the past, such as closed shops in which only union members can work and collective bargain. The act also set up the National Labor Relations Board (NLRB) to enforce its provisions
Fair Labor Standards Act of 1938	This banned child labor and set a minimum wage.
Social Security Act	This act established a system that provided old-age pensions for workers, survivor's benefits for victims of industrial accidents, unemployment insurance, and aid for defendant mothers and children, the blind and physically disabled.[19]

We don't need to wait for another Great Depression in order to fix the problems of this country. We only need leaders who truly believe in the soul of the American Spirit, not in the lust of robber barons.

Democrats have cleaned up the mess left by Republicans for decades, from FDR to Bill Clinton. **Now is the time to clean house once more.**

Now that you know better, what are you going to do about it?

- Get involved?
- Demand accountability?
- Run for office?

- Throw out the GOP?
- Encourage the Democratic leadership to pledge to *The New American Compact?*

The correct answer is *"all of the above."*

Make the decision whether or not <u>you</u> own this country, and then own the decision.

Notes

[1] Medscape; "Public Health Experts Criticize Insurance Benefits Offered by Retail Giant Wal-Mart"; by Melissa Schorr; Nov. 19, 2003

[2] Los Angeles Times; "Big Pharma's Dirty Little Secret"; By Peter Rost; December 26, 2004

[3] Editor and Publisher; "Armstrong Williams' Column Axed by TMS"; By Dave Astor; January 07, 2005

[4] Washington Post; "White House slammed for creating fake news"; By Ceci Connolly; January 08, 2005

[5] The New York Observer; "'Liberal' media silent about Guckert saga"; by Joe Conason; 02.16.05

[6] The Twilight of Democracy; by Patrick E. Kennon; Doubleday, 1995; 308 pages; ISBN 0-385-47539-X

[7] Pat Robertson in a personal letter to Frank Banko, 1992

[8] The Christian Science Monitor; "Commerce in church: faith-based enterprise or unholy invasion?"; By G. Jeffrey MacDonald; December 29, 2004

[9] Matthew 5:1

[10] Matthew 5:9

[11] Anton Szandor Lavey, Author of the Satanic Bible

[12] Adolf Hitler; Speech at Munich, February 24, 1939

[13] Adolf Hitler; Speech at the Reichstag, January 30, 1939

[14] Jerry Falwell speaking to a group of 1,500 people at a conference in Kingsport, TN, at the Thomas Road Baptist Church. His message was carried on television nationwide

[15] Petersburg Times, June 26, 1994; Bailey Smith, a founding father of Robertson's Christian Coalition, once told 15,000 people at a Religious Roundtable briefing in Dallas

[16] The Associated Press; "Scalia Says Religion Infuses U.S. Government and History"; By Vera Dobnik; Monday 22 November 2004

[17] Guardian; "Criminals the lot of us"; Scott Ritter; Thursday January 27, 2005

[18] The Most Dangerous Man in America?, by Rob Boston

[19] http://www.bergen.org/AAST/Projects/depression/successes.html

About the Author

Stacey Tallitsch is the Democratic candidate for Congress in Louisiana's First District for 2006. Pledging to serve his country, Stacey has sworn to bring civility back to government. By doing all he can to remove corruption and to hold those accountable who would destroy this country, where the greedy, the bigoted and the war profiteer, will find no safe haven.

Stacey Tallitsch seeks to lead the charge with a list of progressive issues that have been largely ignored by the general media. Starting with the Religious Right, Stacey is picking battles he chooses, not the other way around.

www.ingramcontent.com/pod-product-compliance
Lightning Source LLC
Chambersburg PA
CBHW031233280526
45784CB00004B/1561